Microsoft System Center Orchestrator 2012 R2 Essentials

Design, implement, and improve your infrastructure administration with System Center Orchestrator 2012 R2's automation process

Miguel Oliveira

BIRMINGHAM - MUMBAI

Microsoft System Center Orchestrator 2012 R2 Essentials

First published: August 2015

Production reference: 1040815

Published by Packt Publishing Ltd.
Livery Place
35 Livery Street
Birmingham B3 2PB, UK.

ISBN 978-1-78528-758-9

www.packtpub.com

Credits

Author
Miguel Oliveira

Reviewers
Ibrahim Aladwan
Jakob Gottlieb Svendsen

Commissioning Editor
Veena Pagare

Acquisition Editor
Vinay Argekar

Content Development Editor
Nikhil Potdukhe

Technical Editor
Deepti Tuscano

Copy Editor
Merilyn Pereira

Project Coordinator
Vijay Kushlani

Proofreader
Safis Editing

Indexer
Tejal Soni

Production Coordinator
Melwyn D'sa

Cover Work
Melwyn D'sa

About the Author

Miguel Oliveira is a versatile IT architect, system engineer, and information security enthusiast who has been living in Switzerland since 2012; before then, he lived in Portugal. During that time, Miguel worked mostly as an IT consultant, having worked with the major companies in Portugal (namely Novabase and Microsoft) with which he designed, developed, and implemented several System Center solutions across different clients, from the banking/financial industry to energy/oil companies. In Switzerland, he worked for international organizations and for a private company as an infrastructure architect and as a senior systems engineer at the time of publishing this book.

Miguel's experience in IT started early as huge curiosity developed in him when he was very young, and it hasn't stopped ever since. The will to develop his knowledge was so strong that at the age of 16, he had his own server at home, and with it, he achieved the first step of his career as an IT systems administrator in 2003, making him an expert on Microsoft products today. He also has good knowledge of VMware, Unix, Network, and Security, which he uses in his daily tasks as an infrastructure architect providing insight and expertise for solutions that are requested by his company.

This book is Miguel's first ever published book, and it has been an amazing and interesting adventure.

Acknowledgments

I would like to thank my wife, Rita, for all her help and support during moments when I wasn't around due to writing this book. I would like to dedicate this book to my little girl, Alice, who has inspired me to do it. I also want to express my gratitude and thanks to Vinay Argekar for giving me the opportunity to author this book and all his patience with me; without him, this book wouldn't have been here.

I also want to thank all my mentors and dear friends who helped me improve over the years: Adalberto Aguiar, Pedro Almeida, Jaime Pocinho, Alberto Nunes, and last but not least, Paulo Lopes. Without these gentlemen, I wouldn't have reached the point of excellence I am at today. Also, a word to my dear friends who kept pushing me to finish the book (you're too many to be listed): a big thank you!

About the Reviewers

Ibrahim Aladwan is a senior systems engineer at STS Jordan, working with Systems Management, Monitoring, Orchestration, the private cloud, and Data Center Virtualization. He has extensive experience as a design and technical expert for complex IT projects in Active Directory, Messaging, Server Virtualization, Desktop Virtualization, System Management, Protection, and Storage Systems with all Implementation Scenarios and Disaster Recovery Solutions. Ibrahim has good training and presentation skills and has consulted, supported, and trained many IT professionals. In addition, he has his own blog and posts, which he feels will be helpful for IT professionals. Ibrahim is currently certified with several Microsoft technologies, such as MCSE:Private Cloud, MCSA:Office 365, Desktop Virtualization, Active Directory, Exchange, and Windows Server.

Jakob Gottlieb Svendsen is a senior consultant, trainer, and chief developer at Coretech A/S, a System Center Gold Partner, and he is a member of the System Center Alliance. Since starting at Coretech in 2007, he has worked on scripting and development and has also worked on developing tools, extensions, and scripts for System Center. His primary focus is Automation, including Orchestrator, Service Management Automation, and Azure Automation. He has presented at TechEd and many other events. Jakob is the cofounder of the Danish PowerShell User Group (`www.psug.dk`). He has authored several courses and blogs at `http://blog.coretech.dk/jgs`.

www.PacktPub.com

Support files, eBooks, discount offers, and more

For support files and downloads related to your book, please visit www.PacktPub.com.

Did you know that Packt offers eBook versions of every book published, with PDF and ePub files available? You can upgrade to the eBook version at www.PacktPub.com and as a print book customer, you are entitled to a discount on the eBook copy. Get in touch with us at service@packtpub.com for more details.

At www.PacktPub.com, you can also read a collection of free technical articles, sign up for a range of free newsletters and receive exclusive discounts and offers on Packt books and eBooks.

https://www2.packtpub.com/books/subscription/packtlib

Do you need instant solutions to your IT questions? PacktLib is Packt's online digital book library. Here, you can search, access, and read Packt's entire library of books.

Why subscribe?

- Fully searchable across every book published by Packt
- Copy and paste, print, and bookmark content
- On demand and accessible via a web browser

Free access for Packt account holders

If you have an account with Packt at www.PacktPub.com, you can use this to access PacktLib today and view 9 entirely free books. Simply use your login credentials for immediate access.

Instant updates on new Packt books

Get notified! Find out when new books are published by following @PacktEnterprise on Twitter or the *Packt Enterprise* Facebook page.

Table of Contents

Preface

In the IT administration world, there has always been a huge demand for quicker ways of doing more with less (either time or material). An IT admin is constantly confronted with requests that either become a routine task and end up increasing their workload, or are just requests that bring a bit more inertia to the daily administrative process by adding either another component to manage, or requests to approve moving forward by looking into another console to monitor in order to take action to move forward. With technology always evolving and becoming more dynamic, IT administration becomes more difficult and demanding, which leads to newer software, tool implementation that will possibly need operations and tasks to be performed on a daily basis and information to be processed and debugged at several levels, exhausting the IT personnel resources on these administrative tasks and, or recurring actions that derivate from all this.

Microsoft System Center Orchestrator 2012 R2 can bring added value and make the IT admin's life easier by cutting short recurrent actions and allowing the IT admin to be focused on other tasks while Orchestrator carries on with those recurrent tasks. We identify and orchestrate these tasks through a workflow in order to make it more autonomous and only intervene when the workflow is not able to work out the task in it.

What is Microsoft System Center Orchestrator 2012 R2?

Microsoft System Center Orchestrator (SCORCH or Orchestrator, from now on) is a workflow automation software that allows IT administrators to automate monitoring and deployment tasks. Orchestrator's tasks are actually Runbooks that are designed through a drag-and-drop user interface and then translates them into .NET, PowerShell, or SSH commands to automate the tasks defined. It is possible to manage various System Center components, as well as AD and other technologies through the use of Integration Packs and can also be used to automate tasks in other operating systems.

This product comes with the Microsoft System Center Suite product family, following a name change from Opalis, which was acquired by Microsoft in December 2009.

We can integrate Orchestrator with other technologies through the use of Integration Packs or by using the Integration Toolkit. We can also develop our own Integration Pack and allow another technology to be managed by our Orchestrator environment, as well as interact with Orchestrator through a web service.

What this book covers

This book covers the many aspects of Orchestrator 2012 R2, including a successful deployment, Runbook design, best practices, how and what to use to develop your own Integration Pack, as well as how to integrate existing ones.

Chapter 1, Configuring and Deploying Orchestrator 2012 R2, covers the infrastructure design aspect of Orchestrator 2012 R2 in a corporate environment, from a simple deployment with an all-in-one server to a more redundant and complex deployment, while we address the prerequisites, firewall ports, and other aspects of the configuration.

Chapter 2, Runbook Designer, focuses on the Runbook Designer. This will be the most used part for the IT administrator, creating the workflows and automatisms, and therefore, we'll address everything there is to know about the Runbook Designer component of Orchestrator 2012 R2.

Chapter 3, Orchestrator Integration Packs, covers the Orchestrator Integration Packs, how they work, and what they are, as well as importing some to our environment for the upcoming chapters.

Chapter 4, Extending Orchestrator, is all about how and where we'll address the Orchestrator capabilities of expansion and the services that surround it. We'll address, in more detail, the different ways that Orchestrator can be accessed and through which methods it can be extended in its capabilities. We'll also verify in more depth the best practices for these expansions, impacts, and troubleshooting scenarios.

Chapter 5, Runbook Examples, covers a series of sample Runbooks that are going to be explored and will serve as a base for you to create your own for the tasks you'll need to cover in your environment. The Runbooks that we're going to address at this point are going to be interconnected with their Integration Packs directly, therefore giving you a good understanding of how to work with them.

Chapter 6, Maintaining an Orchestrator Infrastructure, talks about maintenance being necessary to keep our Orchestrator happy and running. Troubleshooting will also be addressed, as well as backup and recovery.

What you need for this book

To follow this book and get yourself to expert pace, you'll need at least one server with System Center Orchestrator 2012 R2 and all the related technologies:

- Microsoft Active Directory 2008 R2 or above
- System Center Orchestrator 2012 R2

Who this book is for

The audience of this book is skilled IT professionals who work on a daily basis with Active Directory, System Center products, and manage the core of the Data Center infrastructure services and would like to improve or minimize their workload by implementing IT automation processes through Runbooks. It's expected you have a very good knowledge and be at ease with technical terminology, especially regarding those that directly concern Orchestrator such as Active Directory, SQL, IIS, PowerShell, and operating system.

The goal of this book is to give the reader a quick introduction to Orchestrator and take the reader's knowledge to the next level reaching expert level at designing, administering, and troubleshooting Orchestrator.

Conventions

In this book, you will find a number of text styles that distinguish between different kinds of information. Here are some examples of these styles and an explanation of their meaning.

Code words in text, database table names, folder names, filenames, file extensions, pathnames, dummy URLs, user input, and Twitter handles are shown as follows: "In any case, you need to verify the installation logs; they will be under `C:\Users\<USER>\AppData\Local\Microsoft System Center 2012\ Orchestrator\Logs`."

Any command-line input or output is written as follows:

```
Import-Module ServerManager
Add-WindowsFeature NET-Framework-Core –source D:\Sources\sxs
```

New terms and **important words** are shown in bold. Words that you see on the screen, for example, in menus or dialog boxes, appear in the text like this: " Select **Install** on the **System Center 2012 R2 Orchestrator Setup** section of the wizard."

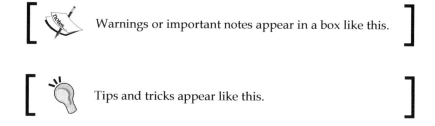

> Warnings or important notes appear in a box like this.

> Tips and tricks appear like this.

Reader feedback

Feedback from our readers is always welcome. Let us know what you think about this book—what you liked or disliked. Reader feedback is important for us as it helps us develop titles that you will really get the most out of.

To send us general feedback, simply e-mail `feedback@packtpub.com`, and mention the book's title in the subject of your message.

If there is a topic that you have expertise in and you are interested in either writing or contributing to a book, see our author guide at `www.packtpub.com/authors`.

Customer support

Now that you are the proud owner of a Packt book, we have a number of things to help you to get the most from your purchase.

Downloading the color images of this book

We also provide you with a PDF file that has color images of the screenshots/diagrams used in this book. The color images will help you better understand the changes in the output. You can download this file from `http://www.packtpub.com/sites/default/files/downloads/7589EN_ColorImages.pdf`.

Errata

Although we have taken every care to ensure the accuracy of our content, mistakes do happen. If you find a mistake in one of our books—maybe a mistake in the text or the code—we would be grateful if you could report this to us. By doing so, you can save other readers from frustration and help us improve subsequent versions of this book. If you find any errata, please report them by visiting `http://www.packtpub.com/submit-errata`, selecting your book, clicking on the **Errata Submission Form** link, and entering the details of your errata. Once your errata are verified, your submission will be accepted and the errata will be uploaded to our website or added to any list of existing errata under the Errata section of that title.

To view the previously submitted errata, go to `https://www.packtpub.com/books/content/support` and enter the name of the book in the search field. The required information will appear under the **Errata** section.

Piracy

Piracy of copyrighted material on the Internet is an ongoing problem across all media. At Packt, we take the protection of our copyright and licenses very seriously. If you come across any illegal copies of our works in any form on the Internet, please provide us with the location address or website name immediately so that we can pursue a remedy.

Please contact us at `copyright@packtpub.com` with a link to the suspected pirated material.

We appreciate your help in protecting our authors and our ability to bring you valuable content.

Questions

If you have a problem with any aspect of this book, you can contact us at questions@packtpub.com, and we will do our best to address the problem.

1
Configuring and Deploying Orchestrator 2012 R2

This chapter will target the goal of having a proper Microsoft System Center Orchestrator 2012 R2 (SCORCH or Orchestrator) architecture in place. We're going to cover the Orchestrator components, their capability to be scalable, and their requirement to better address the question of the design to be chosen. By the end of this chapter, you will be able to identify what requirements you should keep in mind and assess before drawing or implementing Orchestrator.

Microsoft System Center Orchestrator 2012 R2 is a workflow automation product that interconnects with multiple technologies. With Orchestrator, you can target the following points in your datacenter:

- Automation of repeated tasks (either system or manually triggered)
- Interaction between products

The expected result of the automation of repeated tasks is for the administrative workload to be reduced, thereby improving the quality and performance of the IT staff and also improving on the datacenter dynamics.

In this opening chapter, we will address the following points:

- Planning the Orchestrator architecture and deployment
- Deploying a single-server solution
- Deploying a multiple server solution

An overview of the Orchestrator components

To better understand Orchestrator, we need to know the basics of it. We can start off with the fact that it has seven components. The automated workflow is called a **Runbook**. The seven components are as follows:

- **Management Server**: This component coordinates the communication in the Orchestrator architecture between all the other components and it cannot be redundant as there can be only one Management Server per Orchestrator deployment.

- **Orchestrator Database**: As the name suggests, this is composed of a database that will be stored in a Microsoft SQL Server, and it will keep all the Runbooks in it, the status of those Runbooks, and keep the security delegation in place.

- **Runbook Server**: This is the component responsible for executing the Runbooks instances. When a Runbook is invoked, a copy of it is transmitted from the database into the Runbook Server, and then it's executed. The first Runbook Server to get installed gets the primary role.

- **Runbook Designer**: This component is the interface between you and the Orchestrator engine for creating the Runbooks. It has a subcomponent called Runbook Tester for you to use in order to validate the Runbooks you create.

- **Orchestrator Console**: This is a console that runs on Silverlight that uses the Orchestrator Web Service to communicate with Orchestrator.

- **Orchestrator Web Service**: This is the interface that allows applications to connect with Orchestrator and allows them to perform tasks through it, such as starting and stopping Runbooks, or viewing the status.

- **Orchestrator Deployment Manager**: The Deployment Manager is a tool used to deploy **Integration Packs (IPs)**, Runbook servers, and Runbook Designers. This is a subcomponent of the Management Server.

Planning the Orchestrator architecture

The architecture of Orchestrator is, at its base, quite simple and light. At the very beginning you'll find yourself in need of a multiple server Orchestrator deployment for performance and High Availability, and in the end, apart from the High Availability, you won't feel the need for a big Orchestrator infrastructure.

At this point, we'll address a single-server architecture with the database in a separate SQL cluster. For this, the requirements are as follows:

- RAM: 1 GB (recommended 2 GB)
- Disk: 200 MB (available disk space)
- CPU: Dual-core Intel CPU, 2.1 Ghz (or above)
- OS: Windows Server 2008 R2 (with IIS, .NET 3.5 SP1, .NET 4.5, and Silverlight) or above
- SQL Server: Microsoft SQL Server 2008 R2 or above (with Collation: `SQL_Latin1_General_CP1_CI_AS` and Database Engine Service only)

As you can see, the requirements for the Orchestrator architecture following a single-server deployment are not really that demanding. However, let's observe the requirements per component for a multi-server deployment:

- Management server:
  - RAM: 1 GB (recommended 2 GB)
  - Disk: 200 MB (available disk space)
  - CPU: Dual-core Intel CPU, 2.1 Ghz or above
  - OS: Windows Server 2008 R2 (.NET 3.5 SP1) or above

- Orchestrator database:
  - SQL Server: Microsoft SQL Server 2008 R2 or above
  - Collation: `SQL_Latin1_General_CP1_CI_AS`
  - SQL Roles: Database Engine
  - Location: Local or Remote (cluster supported)

- Runbook server:
  - RAM: 1 GB (recommended 2 GB)
  - Disk: 200 MB (available disk space)
  - CPU: Dual-core Intel CPU, 2.1 Ghz or above
  - OS: Windows Server 2008 R2 (.NET 3.5 SP1) or above

- Runbook designer:
  - RAM: 1 GB (recommended 2 GB)
  - Disk: 200 MB (available disk space)
  - CPU: Dual-core Intel CPU, 2.1 Ghz or above
  - OS: Windows Server 2008 R2, Windows 7 SP1 or above

- Orchestration console / Web service server:
  - ○ RAM: 1 GB (recommended 2 GB)
  - ○ Disk: 200 MB (available disk space)
  - ○ CPU: Dual-core Intel CPU, 2.1 Ghz or above
  - ○ OS: Windows Server 2008 R2 (.NET 3.5 SP1, .NET 4.5, IIS, Silverlight) or above

Usually, the multi-server deployments are in fact connected to the High Availability questions, but keep with mind that the Management Server is a single component that can't be deployed in High Availability, even though the Runbook Servers are able to execute the Runbooks without that component.

On the **Active Directory (AD)** side, you'll need to also fulfill some requirements:

User/Group	Name	Type	Comments
User	DOMAIN\scorchmssvc	Service account	This is the main management server's service account and it will be granted a logon as a service during the installation. It is also used for the Monitor service.
User	DOMAIN\scorchrbsvc	Service account	This is the account used for accessing resources that are specified on the Runbooks. This account might require access to remote computers.
Group	DOMAIN\Scorch_Users	Group	Users Security Global Group for allowing default access to Orchestrator
Group	DOMAIN\Scorch_Ops	Group	Operators Security Group to allow access as the Runbook operator on Orchestrator
Group	DOMAIN\Scorch_Admins	Group	This is the Full Administration Security Group for Orchestrator

The next screenshot shows these accounts and groups in Active Directory, and in the end you should have something quite similar in your environment. The users and groups don't need to be named exactly the same as the examples we give here; they can be adapted to your standards, but keep these in mind for your reference for the rest of this book.

Name	Type	Description
scorchrbsvc	User	Orchestrator Runbook Server Service Account
scorchmssvc	User	Orchestrator Management Server Service Account
Scorch_Users	Group	Orchestrator Console Users
Scorch_Ops	Group	Orchestrator Runbook Creators
Scorch_Admins	Group	Orchestrator Full Admins

On the network side, we'll need the following exceptions on the firewall:

Source	Target	Default Port (TCP)	Notes
Runbook Designer	Management Server	135, 1024-65535	The Runbook Designer communicates with the management server over DCOM; by default, the DCOM uses port 135 to initiate the connection and then moves to a dynamic port between 1024 and 65535.
Management Server / Runbook Server / Web Service	Orchestration Database	1433	This takes care of the Microsoft SQL Server connectivity.
Client Browser	Orchestrator REST-based web service	81	These are ports used for connecting to the Orchestration console.
	Orchestration console	82	

All the ports above can be configured to better suit your environment.

Now, in terms of the scalability of the Orchestrator, we can have redundancy in the Orchestrator Web Service / Console, Runbook Servers, and Orchestrator Database. However, we won't be able to have more than one Management Server.

You might consider having the components divided between servers due to service availability, but there's also the Runbooks workload expected and the number of simultaneous Runbooks that you'll have running to consider, as well as their importance.

Our advice would be to have one single-server deployed for the Runbooks development and preparation, and then for production, a redundant deployment of Runbook Server, Orchestrator Web Service / Console Server, and the Orchestrator Database under a SQL cluster. This way, you'll cover any need of simultaneously executing some Runbooks and High Availability.

Good! Now that we've defined all the requirements, and since all are in place, we'll do a sanity check so we can see if we're ready to go forward.

So, to move on to the next point, on installing the Orchestrator architecture you've decided to go with, you'll need to achieve the following steps:

1. Create Active Directory accounts:
    ◦   Service accounts
    ◦   AD groups

2. Install an operating system:
    ◦   Windows Server (2008 R2 or above)
    ◦   Add it to the domain
    ◦   Add service accounts to the administrator's local group
    ◦   Add the Orchestrator administrators group to the administrator's local group

3. Configure OS roles and features:
    ◦   IIS
    ◦   .NET 3.5 SP1
    ◦   .NET 4.5
    ◦   Silverlight

Don't forget that some of the OS roles and features are only required for some of the Orchestrator components. Check the list to see which component needs which piece of software.

Also, it's not on this list, but we're assuming you have a SQL cluster or a single-server in place to accommodate your Orchestrator database. Don't forget the permissions on that SQL server for the account running the Management Server.

The OS roles and features prerequisites can all be installed using PowerShell in order to achieve a faster single-server deployment. In order to do so, you can execute the following command:

```
Import-Module ServerManager

Add-WindowsFeature NET-Framework-Core,NET-Framework-45-ASPNET,NET-
WCF-Services45,NET-WCF-HTTP-Activation45,NET-WCF-TCP-
PortSharing45,Web-Server,Web-WebServer,Web-Common-Http,Web-Default-
Doc,Web-Dir-Browsing,Web-Http-Errors,Web-Static-Content,Web-
Health,Web-Http-Logging,Web-Log-Libraries,Web-Request-Monitor,Web-
Http-Tracing,Web-Performance,Web-Stat-Compression,Web-Security,Web-
Filtering,Web-Digest-Auth,Web-Windows-Auth,Web-App-Dev,Web-Net-
Ext,Web-Net-Ext45,Web-Asp-Net,Web-Asp-Net45,Web-CGI,Web-ISAPI-
Ext,Web-ISAPI-Filter,Web-Mgmt-Tools,Web-Mgmt-Console -source
D:\Sources\sxs
```

Deploying a single-server solution

As discussed in the previous section, we can use a single-server to host all the components of Orchestrator if we're targeting a small environment and/or we have the objective of having an Orchestrator for the development and quality assessment of our Runbooks before getting them into production. If you jumped straight into this part, we strongly suggest you read the *Planning the Orchestrator architecture* section before proceeding.

As of the time of writing, Windows Server 2012 R2 has been out for quite a while and it's the OS selected to host our Orchestrator. So, once you have chosen the OS and deployed it, and after having joined to the domain and having done the basic configurations, we can move on with deploying the prerequisites:

1. Verify that you have permissions on the SQL Server selected to host the database, that the collation is the one specified in the previous section, and finally that **Windows Authentication** is the authentication mechanism selected. If you choose to install the SQL Server locally, don't forget to **get the Database Engine Services options** and the share features by navigating to **Management Tools | Basic**.

2. Add the Orchestrator Administrators group and the Management Service account to the local Administrators group of the server.

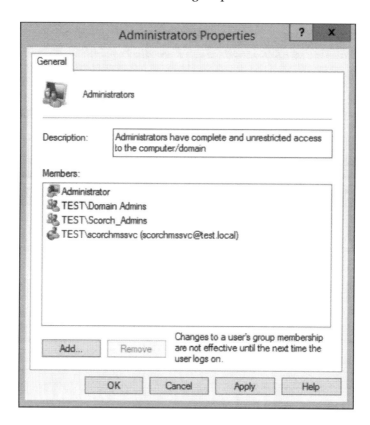

3. Enable the **Web Server (IIS)** role, accept the features added, and proceed with the installation. The default settings of this role will suffice as the Orchestrator will configure it accordingly for you. If the Orchestrator installation doesn't detect this role on the server, it will install it for you.

4. Install the **.NET 3.5 SP1** feature. Don't forget to indicate the alternative source for the installation to occur.

5. (Only if you're installing on Windows Server 2008 R2): Install the **.NET 4.5** feature. If you forget to activate the **ASP.NET** and **HTTP Activation** features, the installer will take care of activating them for you.

6. Install **Silverlight**. If you start the console without installing it, you'll be required to install it.

7. Launch the installation using the `SetupOrchestrator.exe`. Select **Install** on the **System Center 2012 R2 Orchestrator Setup** section of the wizard.

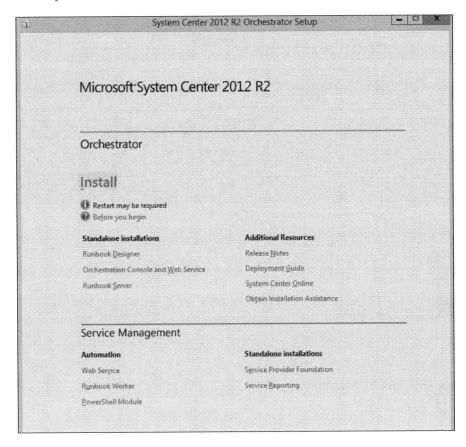

8. On the **Product registration** page, enter your organization's details and product key, and then click on **Next**.

9. Take your time to read the license terms, and if you accept them, continue the installation by clicking on **Next**.

10. On **Select features to install**, by default you'll have all of them selected. As we're installing a single-server, this is the desired selection, so just press **Next**.

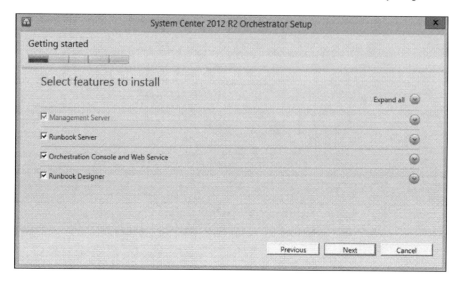

11. As seen in step 4 of this installation, we didn't include the **ASP.NET** features on IIS, so Orchestrator will install them for us (press **Next**) and then it will confirm that everything's OK.

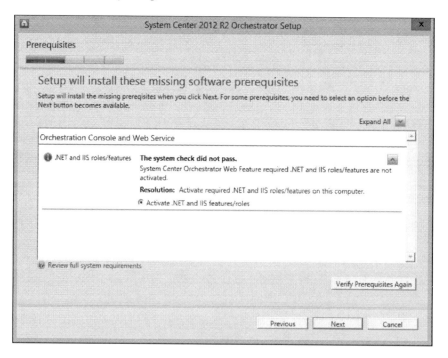

12. At the **Configure the service account** step, we'll use the Management Service `scorchmssvc` account. The explanation on this screen can be a bit misleading, but this is the management service that we're talking about. In a multi-server deployment, this will be different. We'll get there…

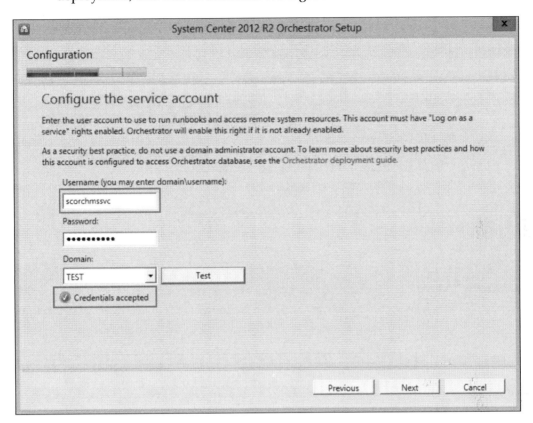

13. Now, at **Configure the database server**, we'll use our server/instance (if any instance), and the port, and we'll verify the connectivity. If everything's OK, we'll move on with **Next**.

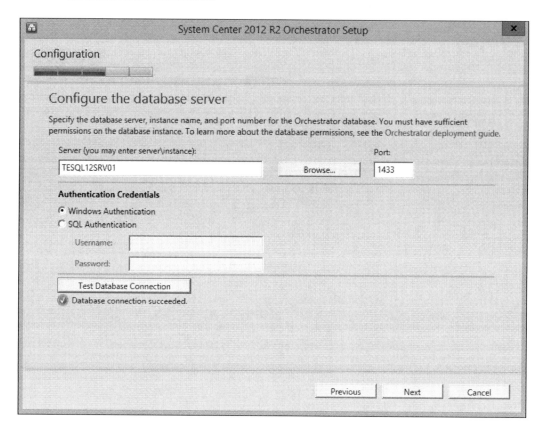

14. Verify the database settings at the **Configure the database** page and specify the database name if you want something different. The default is **Orchestrator**. Proceed with **Next**.

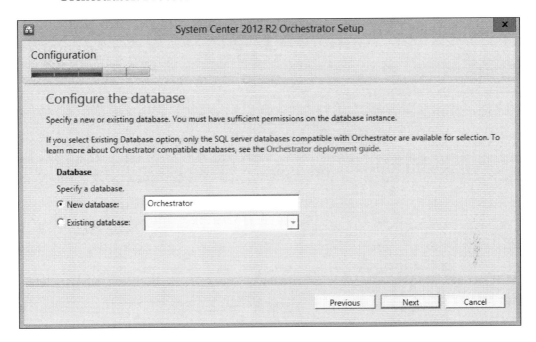

15. Now it's time to **configure Orchestrators users group**, but although the title of the page can be deceiving, this is not the normal users group, but rather the Administrators group. Click on **Browse** and select the proper group that you've defined (**Scorch_Admins** in this example). Click on **Next** when ready.

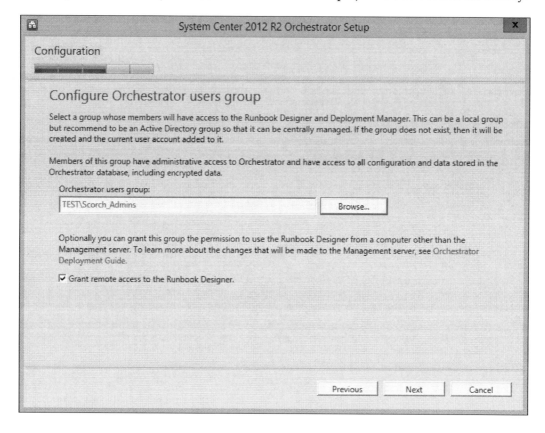

16. At the **Configure the ports for the web services** page, usually the default ports 81 and 82 are OK, but if these ports are not compliant with your environment or you wish to make the service available at some other port, this is the time to do it. If you do change the ports, don't forget to keep them in mind for the rest of this book as we'll use the default ones for every sample and configuration. Push **Next**.

17. Time to select the installation location. Usually, the default is OK, but, once again, you can specify another location that is more suitable for your needs. Push **Next**.

18. On the **Help improve Microsoft System Center Orchestrator,** select the options you prefer and click on **Next**.

19. Review **Installation summary,** and if everything's OK, click on **Install** to start the installation.

20. Once the installation finishes, you'll be given the status of the installation along with a few options to consider before finishing the setup:

    1. Launch Windows Update.

    2. Visit System Center Orchestrator Online.

    3. When the setup closes, start **Runbook Designer.**

All these steps can be automated with Powershell. The following is a sample of the command line to execute in order to install it in an unattended way with the Orchestrator in a single-server:

```
D:\Setup\Setup.exe /DbServer:SQLSERVER\INSTANCE
/DbNameNew:Orchestrator /WebServicePort:81 /WebConsolePort:82
/OrchestratorRemote /UseMicrosoftUpdate:1 /SendCEIPReports:0
/EnableErrorReporting:never /Components:all
/ServiceUserName:DOMAIN\scorchmssvc /ServicePassword:IWontTellYou
/OrchestratorUsersGroup:(Group's SID) /Key:XXXXX-XXXXX-XXXX-XXXX-
XXXXX /Silent
```

As we're setting up only one server, we're only going to use the Management Service account for the Management Service and for the Runbook Service. In this type of deployment, only one account is required. The Runbook Server service account will be used for any additional Runbook Servers that we may like to deploy in the future, and it's best practice to separate the two services into separate accounts to avoid a single point of failure in the future.

If you choose to go with the command-line installation, don't forget to retrieve the `Scorch_Admins` group SID. If you don't want to specify the group, it will use the default one locally called `OrchestratorUsersGroup`. If you would like to install Orchestrator into another directory, you can use the `InstallDir()` function and specify the directory.

In any case, you need to verify the installation logs. They will be under `C:\Users\<USER>\AppData\Local\Microsoft System Center 2012\Orchestrator\Logs`.

With this complete, you will have a fully functional Orchestrator 2012 R2 deployment.

Deploying a multi-server solution

As mentioned previously in the *Planning the Orchestrator architecture* section, we can use a multi-server deployment to separately host the components of Orchestrator if we're targeting a highly available environment or if we have a huge demand for Runbooks running at the same time. If you jumped straight into this part, we strongly suggest you read the *Planning the Orchestrator architecture* section before proceeding.

Management Server

On the multi-server solution, we have to start by deploying the Management Server along with the database. This is the main focus point of our Orchestrator architecture, so we have to start with it.

1. Verify that you have permissions on the SQL Server selected to host the database and that the collation is the one specified on the previous section, and, finally, that **Windows Authentication** is the authentication mechanism selected. If you chose to install the SQL Server locally, don't forget to **get the Database Engine Services options**, with the share features by navigating to **Management Tools | Basic**.

2. Add the Orchestrator Administrators group and the Management Service account to the local Administrators group of the server as explained above for the single-server instance.

3. Install the **.NET 3.5 SP1** feature. Don't forget to indicate the alternative source for the installation to occur.

4. (Only if you're installing on Windows Server 2008 R2): Install the **.NET 4.5** feature. You don't need to activate the ASP.NET as this is the Management Server, so it won't need it.

5. Launch the install using `SetupOrchestrator.exe`. Select **Install** on the **System Center 2012 R2 Orchestrator Setup** section of the wizard.

6. On the **Product registration** page, enter your organization's details and product key, and then click on **Next**.

7. Take your time to read the license terms, and if you accept them, continue the installation by clicking on **Next**.

8. On **Select features to install**, by default you'll have all of them selected. We're going to remove all of them except the required one—**Management Server** - and then proceed. Click on **Next**.

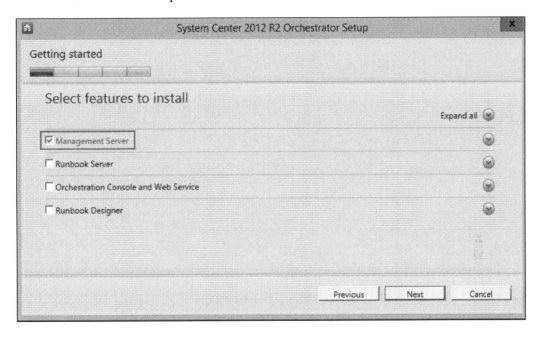

9. At the **Configure the service account** step, we'll use the Management Service (scorchmssvc) account, test, and proceed with **Next**.

10. Now, at **Configure the database server**, we'll use our server/instance (if any instance) and the port, and we'll verify the connectivity. If everything's OK, we'll move on with **Next**.

11. Verify the database settings at the **Configure the database** page and specify the database name if you want something different. The default is **Orchestrator**. Proceed with **Next**.

12. In **Configure Orchestrator users group,** select the group defined earlier for the Orchestrators Admins function, in this case TEST\Scorch_Admins. After this is set, press **Next**.

13. Select the installation location that's most convenient for you and proceed with **Next**.

14. On the **Microsoft Update** screen, select the **On (recommended)** option and proceed with **Next**. It's very important to keep your Orchestrator up to date.

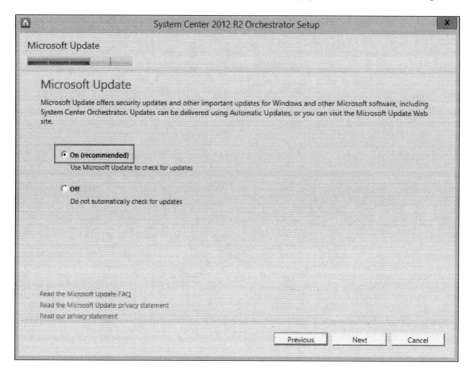

15. On **Help improve Microsoft System Center Orchestrator**, select the option you prefer and proceed with **Next**.

16. On **Installation Summary**, verify your options and proceed with **Install** if they're OK.

17. Once finished, you'll see a **Setup completed successfully** page with two options:

    ◦ Launch Windows Update
    ◦ Visit System Center Orchestrator Online

You'll then have finished your installation. We strongly suggest that you run the **Windows Update** option and update everything there is to update.

If you wish to install the **Management Server** component in an unattended way, don't forget to retrieve the Scorch_Admins group SID. If you don't want to specify the group, it will use the default one locally called OrchestratorUsersGroup. If you would like to install Orchestrator into another directory, you can use the InstallDir function and specify the directory.

In any case, you need to verify the installation logs. They will be under `C:\Users\<USER>\AppData\Local\Microsoft System Center 2012\Orchestrator\Logs`. You can do the unattended installation by executing the following commands:

```
Import-Module ServerManager

Add-WindowsFeature NET-Framework-Core -source D:\Sources\sxs

D:\Setup\Setup.exe /DbServer:SQLSERVER\INSTANCE
/DbNameNew:Orchestrator /OrchestratorRemote /UseMicrosoftUpdate:1
/SendCEIPReports:0 /EnableErrorReporting:never
/Components:ManagementServer /ServiceUserName:DOMAIN\scorchmssvc
/ServicePassword:IWontTellYou /OrchestratorUsersGroup:(Group's SID)
/Key:XXXXX-XXXXX-XXXX-XXXX-XXXXX /Silent
```

Runbook Server

Once you have deployed the Management Server, you can proceed with the next logical step on the installation, that is, the Runbook Server. The Orchestrator architecture needs at least one Runbook Server in order to function.

For the installation of the Runbook Server, these are the steps to take:

1. Have the Management Server installed and the Runbook Server Service account at hand (`scorchrbsvc`).

2. Add the Orchestrator Administrators group, the Management Service account, and the Runbooks Service account to the local Administrators group of the server.

3. Install the **.NET 3.5 SP1** feature. Don't forget to indicate the alternative source for the installation to occur.

4. (Only if you're installing on Windows Server 2008 R2): Install the **.NET 4.5** feature. You don't need to activate the ASP.NET as this is the Runbook Server, so it won't need it.

5. Launch the installation using the `SetupOrchestrator.exe`. Select **Runbook Server** under the **Standalone** installations in the **System Center 2012 R2 Orchestrator Setup** section of the wizard.

6. On the **Product registration** page, enter your organization's details and product key, and then click on **Next**.

7. Take your time to read the license terms, and if you accept them, continue the installation by clicking on **Next**.

8. Click on **Configure the service account** that was created for the Runbook Server service, in this case, `scorchrbsvc`. Proceed after testing by clicking on **Next**.

9. On the **Configure the database server** page, type the same server and instance (if applicable) that you used on the Management Server configuration. Click on **Next**.

10. On **Configure the database**, select the existing database (usually selected by default). Push **Next** to continue.

11. Click on **Select the installation location** and proceed with **Next**.

12. Regarding the **Microsoft Update** page, select your preference and click on **Next**.

13. On **Help improve Microsoft System Center Orchestrator**, select your preferences and proceed with **Next**.

14. Review the **Installation Summary**, and if everything's OK, click **Install** to start the process.

As mentioned previously, we recommend you take the time to get all the latest updates and then carry on with the installation of the other components.

If you prefer to run an unattended installation, you can do so by executing the following commands:

```
Import-Module ServerManager

Add-WindowsFeature NET-Framework-Core -source D:\Sources\sxs

D:\Setup\Setup.exe /DbServer:SQLSERVER\INSTANCE
/DbNameExisting:Orchestrator /UseMicrosoftUpdate:1 /SendCEIPReports:0
/EnableErrorReporting:never /Components:RunbookServer
/ServiceUserName:DOMAIN\scorchmssvc /ServicePassword:IWontTellYou
/Key:XXXXX-XXXXX-XXXX-XXXX-XXXXX /Silent
```

Orchestrator console and web service

After deploying both the Management Server and Runbook Server, you can deploy the console and w service getting the Orchestrator architecture finalized, given that the Runbook Designer will get installed on a Windows 7/8 client. There's no specific order to the installation of the components, except that the Management Server has to be always the first component to get installed.

To install the Console and Web Service, you'll need to execute the following steps:

1. Have the **Management Server** installed and the **Management Server Service account** at hand (`scorchmssvc`).

2. Add the Orchestrator Administrators group, the Management Service account, and the Runbooks Service account to the local Administrators group of the server.

3. Install the **.NET 3.5 SP1** feature. Don't forget to indicate the alternative source for the installation to occur.

4. (Only if you're installing on Windows Server 2008 R2): Install the **.NET 4.5** feature and activate the **ASP.NET** and **HTTP Activation** features. If you forget to activate this feature or don't want to activate it for now, Orchestrator will install it for you during the setup.

5. Install the **Web Server (IIS)** with the default settings.

6. Install **Silverlight**. If you don't install it now, when you get to the **Console**, it will request that you install Silverlight.

7. Launch the installation using `SetupOrchestrator.exe`. Select **Orchestrator Console** and **Web Service** under **Standalone** installations on the **System Center 2012 R2 Orchestrator Setup** section of the wizard.

8. On the **Product registration** page, enter your organization's details and product key, and then click on **Next**.

9. Take your time to read the license terms, and if you accept them, continue the installation by clicking on **Next**.

10. Click on **Configure the service account** that was created for the Management Server service. In this case, `scorchmssvc`. Proceed after testing by clicking on **Next**.

11. On the **Configure the database server** page, type the same server and instance (if applicable) that you used on the **Management Server** configuration. Click on **Next**.

12. On **Configure the database**, select the existing database (usually selected by default). Push **Next** to continue.

13. At the **Configure the ports for the web services** page, usually the default ports `81` and `82` are OK, but if these ports are not compliant with your environment or you wish to make the service available at some other port, this is the time to do it. If you do change the ports, don't forget to keep them in mind for the rest of this book as we'll use the default ones for every sample and configuration. Push **Next**.

14. Click on **Select the installation location** and proceed by clicking on **Next**.

15. On **Help improve Microsoft System Center Orchestrator**, select your preferences and proceed with **Next**.

16. Review the **Installation summary**, and if everything's OK, click on **Install** to start the process.

17. If you want to install the Console and Web Service in an unattended way, you can do so by using the following commands:

```
Import-Module ServerManager

Add-WindowsFeature NET-Framework-Core,NET-Framework-45-
ASPNET,NET-
WCF-Services45,NET-WCF-HTTP-Activation45,NET-WCF-TCP-
PortSharing45,Web-Server,Web-WebServer,Web-Common-Http,Web-
Default-
Doc,Web-Dir-Browsing,Web-Http-Errors,Web-Static-Content,Web-
Health,Web-Http-Logging,Web-Log-Libraries,Web-Request-
Monitor,Web-
Http-Tracing,Web-Performance,Web-Stat-Compression,Web-
Security,Web-
Filtering,Web-Digest-Auth,Web-Windows-Auth,Web-App-Dev,Web-
Net-
Ext,Web-Net-Ext45,Web-Asp-Net,Web-Asp-Net45,Web-CGI,Web-ISAPI-
Ext,Web-ISAPI-Filter,Web-Mgmt-Tools,Web-Mgmt-Console -source
D:\Sources\sxs


D:\Setup\Setup.exe /DbServer:SQLSERVER\INSTANCE
/DbNameExisting:Orchestrator /WebServicePort:81
/WebConsolePort:82 /OrchestratorRemote /SendCEIPReports:0
/EnableErrorReporting:never /Components:WebComponents
/ServiceUserName:DOMAIN\scorchmssvc
/ServicePassword:IWontTellYou /Key:XXXXX-XXXXX-XXXX-XXXX-XXXXX
/Silent
```

That's it for the Orchestrator architecture to be complete on the server side. Now all that's missing is the Runbook Designer that we will install on our Windows 8.1 (or 7) workstation on the multi-server solution.

Runbook Designer

To achieve a successful installation on the Runbook Designer, you'll need to get .NET 3.5 SP1 and Silverlight installed. The Runbook Designer can be installed independently whether or not you have a Management Server and the proper database setup already, but it will be rather useless without it.

Before proceeding with this installation, please complete either a single-server or a multi-server implementation:

1. On the machine selected to install the **Runbook Designer**, enable the feature **.NET 3.5 SP1** (if not already enabled).

2. Install **Silverlight**. If you don't install it now, you'll be prompted to install it if you have access to the console.

3. Launch the installation using the `SetupOrchestrator.exe`. Select **Runbook Designer** under the **Standalone** installations on the **System Center 2012 R2 Orchestrator Setup** section of the wizard.

4. On the **Product registration** page, enter your organization's details and product key, and then click on **Next**.

5. Take your time to read the license terms, and if you accept them, continue the installation by clicking on **Next**.

6. Click on **Select the installation location** and proceed with **Next**.

7. On **Help improve Microsoft System Center Orchestrator**, select your preferences and proceed with **Next**.

8. Review **Installation Summary**, and if everything's OK, click on **Install** to start the process.

9. Once the installation completes, you'll be given the status of the installation along with a few options to consider before finishing the setup:

    1. Launch Windows update.

    2. Visit System Center Orchestrator Online.

    3. When Setup closes, start the Runbook Designers.

10. As with all the other components of Orchestrator, you can also run the Runbook Designer installation in an unattended fashion. For that, you'll need to execute the following commands:

```
Import-Module ServerManager

Add-WindowsFeature NET-Framework-Core –source D:\Sources\sxs


D:\Setup\Setup.exe
/SendCEIPReports:0/EnableErrorReporting:never
/Components:RunbookDesigner /Key:XXXXX-XXXXX-XXXX-XXXX-XXXXX
/Silent
```

When you start the Runbook Designer for the first time from a remote location (a workstation or server that's not the Management Server), you'll be presented with an error message saying **Could not find Orchestrator Management Service on 'WORKSTATION'**.

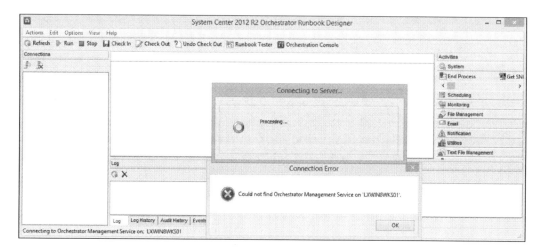

Confirm with **OK,** and then click on **Actions**. Select **Connect...** and insert the **Management Server** name into the box.

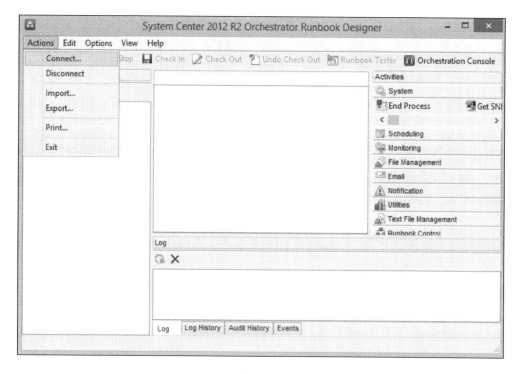

In the **Connection** window, insert the name of the Management Server that you'll be connecting to. This is a one-time setup for your user.

Once connected, you'll see **Runbook Designer** completely available.

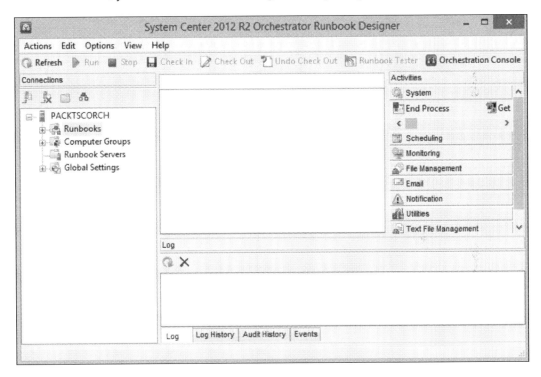

Before you can use the **Orchestrator Console** option in **Runbook Designer,** you'll have to define it. To do so, go to **Options | Orchestrator Console** and insert the proper URL.

In our example here (with the multi-server implementation), the URL is
`http://PACKTSCORCHW:82`.

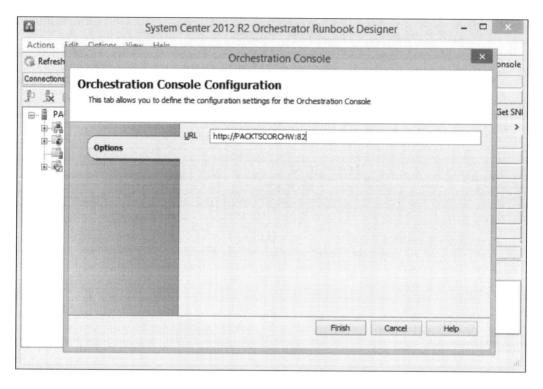

After that, press **Finish** and you'll have everything configured as it should be.

Summary

So far, we've seen how to plan and deploy our Orchestrator architecture and the requirements and prerequisites for deploying successfully each component of Orchestrator in a single-server environment or multi-server environment.

All the actions completed on this chapter are essential for the successful usage of Orchestrator in your environment, so we recommend you plan your Orchestrator architecture thoroughly.

Welcome to Orchestrator! The journey has just begun...

2
Runbook Designer

Now that we've got our environment in place, we can start creating Runbooks with the Runbook Designer. But first, we need to understand what the Runbook Designer is and what to expect from it. At first sight, it might be pretty clear from the name of the component that this is the tool we're going to use to create Runbooks, and although that's true, it's not only that. We'll see this further in this chapter. Let's dig in!

In this chapter, we will address the following points:

- The Runbook Designer overview
- The Runbooks overview
- Creation of a Runbook
- Testing a Runbook on the Runbook Designer

 Before you start your Runbook Designer, don't forget that if you're starting it from another machine that's not the Management Server, you'll need to configure the proper server to connect to. Refer to the previous chapter on the *Runbook Designer* section for more details.

Runbook Designer overview

Let's get to know the Runbook Designer tool better, as it will be where we'll spend most of our time while creating our Orchestrations.

We'll introduce you to each component of Runbook Designer, and you'll need to know them by heart to not feel lost further into this book as we'll be using a lot of these names.

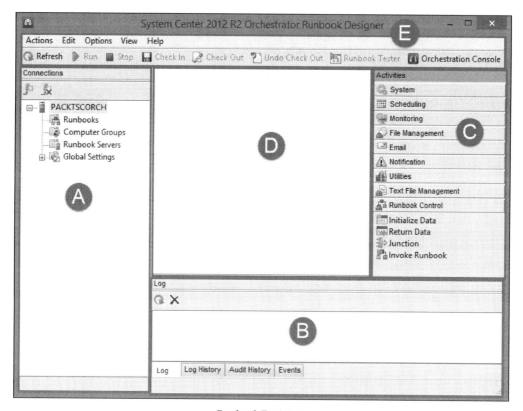

Runbook Designer

Let's get to know the Runbook Designer better. For that, you'll need to understand the panes in the preceding screenshot. They are explained as follows:

- **A**: The **Connections** pane is for general connection and server settings, and this is where you'll navigate between folders that will contain Runbooks. Under **Computer Groups**, the folders will serve to arrange **Computer Groups** themselves.

- **B**: The Runbook logging pane is for Runbook-specific logs and events.

- **C**: The **Activities** pane is where you'll have all the activities that you can include into your Runbooks on the central pane.

- **D**: The central pane is where you'll be building and defining your Runbooks.

- **E**: The commands and menu bar follows the Microsoft philosophy of MMC. This is where all the commands and menus are arranged.

As we go through the following chapters, you'll be working more and more with these components of the Runbook Designer, so get to know them better. In order to do this, we'll see some of these components a bit more in detail.

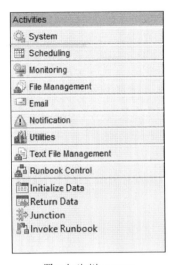

The Activities pane

The **Activities** pane has all the available activities listed under each category. This allows you to drag and drop each activity into the Runbook you're designing.

From a fresh installation of Orchestrator, you'll get the standard available activities. These are the activities that come out of the box with Orchestrator, and you don't need to install any integration pack in order to get them.

The activities are separated into categories to allow better access and a faster search of the activities you need for your Runbook.

As an example, you can see that the **Runbook Control** category has four activities. Apart from this specific category, all the other categories have their own activities and we will be using some of them for sure and even adding more with integration packs.

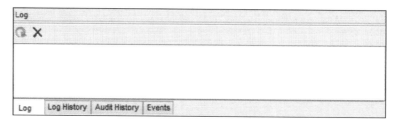

The Log pane

The **Log** pane allows access to all the specific log files from Orchestrator regarding Runbooks, and it can become quite handy when troubleshooting issues arise. There are four types of logs here that we can access directly:

- **Log**: This shows information about running Runbook instances at that moment.

- **Log History**: This displays historical information about Runbook instances.

- **Audit History**: This shows information about changes made to Runbooks. You can retrieve the who, when, and what information in this log.

- **Events**: This will show the information, warnings, or errors about the connections from the Runbook Designer to the Management Server, Runbook servers, and the database.

These logs are all stored in the Orchestrator database, and it's through the Runbook Designer that you'll access them, although you can also access them from the **Orchestration Console**.

To limit the amount of data retained from the logs in the database, you can configure the **Log Purge** option. This is a good idea because, as you're using the Runbook Designer to access the information, the bigger the logs are, the slower the designer will be. Keep them at a reasonable level where you won't lose much information about the latest actions but in a way that it doesn't impact the performance of the Runbook Designer either.

The **Log Purge** has a daily purge at 1:00 A.M. by default and will keep the last 5000 entries until it runs at that time, and from there it will only keep the most recent 500 entries. You can change these settings by right-clicking on the **Management Server** in the Runbook Designer and selecting **Log Purge**. Then, you'll have your options to configure.

Commands and menu bar

On the commands and menu bar, you'll find a few options that are quite important and we're going to address them for your understanding.

Most of the these commands focus on the Runbooks and are to be used with them, specifically, **Run**, **Stop**, **Check In**, **Check Out**, **Undo Check Out**, and **Runbook Tester**.

Let's detail these commands:

- **Run**: This command allows you to trigger the Runbook you have selected the moment you press it. You'll be essentially executing the Runbook, and this will trigger all the requests for information, monitoring, and other activities you've included in your Runbook.

- **Stop**: As the name indicates, it will terminate the Runbook execution.

- **Check In**: This option will commit the changes you make to a Runbook and save them into the database. It also releases the Runbook you were editing for other users to edit.

- **Check Out**: This option blocks the Runbook by putting it into the edit mode and locking it from being edited by other users.

- **Undo Check Out**: This will revert the Runbook to the status it had before the last time you checked out. This will be handy if you find out that the latest version of your Runbook is not functioning properly and you want to revert to a working.

- **Runbook Tester**: This is the tool we will use to test our Runbooks before releasing them into the production.

One other aspect of the Runbook Designer is that you can open **Orchestration Console** from here. All you need to do is to configure it (check the Runbook Designer installation in *Chapter 1, Configuring and Deploying Orchestrator 2012 R2*) and then, when you use the command in your Runbook Designer, you'll be automatically redirected to the browser with the proper address.

There is still the **Runbook Tester** to address, but to better address this part, we'll need to have a Runbook created, so we'll switch over into Runbooks and we'll come back to finish the test after knowing more about the Runbooks.

Runbooks overview

OK, so we've been talking a lot about Runbooks, but we haven't really discussed them in depth. Well, it's time to do that! We've included this part in the middle of the *Runbook Designer* section because they are both so interconnected that it will be easier and more practical to address them together, while maintaining focus over the Runbook itself.

Before we start building Runbooks, we need to understand the basics that are related to concepts, design principles, and understanding the fundamental building blocks of Runbooks.

These are shown in the following list:

- Naming, version management, and folders
- Smart links
- Published data and the data bus
- Global settings (counters, variables, and schedules)
- Subscription and data manipulation
- Looping
- Runbook control
- Runbook design recommendations

Naming, version management, and folders

There's no best practice in terms of Runbook management and organization, so it's up to you to define how you want to keep your Runbooks organized. So the following point is our recommendation, and we believe that by adopting it you will save time and effort while managing and maintaining your Runbooks.

The following screenshot shows which strategy we should use to organize our Runbooks at work, and we've come up with this structure by having discussions within the system administrators group in order to reach a common understanding.

So in order to keep a rational tracking of our Runbooks, we navigate to **Technology | Task | Process | Version**, and in this way, we keep a sane delegation and we can also track all the changes we made, back and forth, under a certain process we've automated.

This way, it is also possible to delegate administration over the **Task | Process** we have created on our Runbook Designer.

Don't forget to also keep a good naming convention on your Runbook activities; this way you can avoid confusion on repeated tasks (as in the example in the following image):

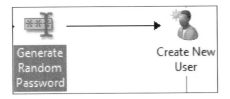

It will be very helpful to keep a good naming convention for all objects within Orchestrator, and also, a good description whenever necessary or possible will help you and your team understand what they have before them.

Smart links

In this same preceding image, you'll notice that there is an arrow between activities; this is called a smart link and it will be heavily used through the creation of Runbooks as every activity needs a link that will lead to the next one.

The smart link is customizable in terms of look and feel. To get into the customization of it, you'll need to go to **Options | Configure** and then proceed with the available options.

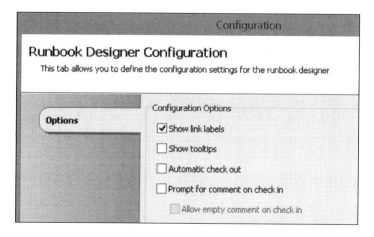

In order to understand these options, we'll address them one by one so you can get a good understanding of what each one of them does:

- **Show link labels**: This displays the name of each link. This text comes from the **Name** field on the **General** tab of the link's **Properties** dialog box.

- **Show tooltips**: This displays tooltips when you hover your cursor over an object in a Runbook. This text comes from the **Description** field on the **General** tab of the object's **Properties** dialog box.

- **Automatic check out**: This automatically checks out a Runbook when you begin to edit it. If not selected, you are prompted whether you want to check out the Runbook.

- **Prompt for comment on check in**: This displays the **Comment** dialog box when you check in a Runbook.

- **Allow empty comment on check in**: As the name indicates, it allows Runbooks to be checked in without filling the comments section.

You can also change the color and thickness of each smart link in Orchestrator. This will help you have better visualization of the path to follow in case you're making changes to your Runbook.

Now, why are they called smart links? That's a good question. They're called smart links because when you open the properties of a link you'll have the **Include** and **Exclude** conditions; these will either pass to the next activity or not. These conditions present a lot of possibilities to make certain checks before proceeding to the next activity.

Along with the possibilities explained previously, we can also use these conditions in order to trigger multiple paths on our Runbook and have multiple activities executing at the same time, depending on a certain condition! Remember that Runbooks can run a single activity or multiple activities at a time.

You can also use regular expressions in these conditions for input validation to check whether the data input obeys certain rules or not.

Published data and the Data bus

At this point down the road, we know that all activities will generate data that is *published* when the activity runs, and that becomes available to any other activity in the Runbook. We call the data that the activity publishes **Published Data**, and we call the *media* used to transport it the **Data bus**. The **Data bus** is the mechanism that serves as the information carrier between activities in a Runbook.

Within the **Published Data**, we have specific data that comes out from the executed activity with the data retrieved from those fields and is then assembled with the next activity and consequent activity specific published data. You can then, in certain activities, use the **Published Data** to populate necessary fields of action that will use the information to process and execute the activity steps.

As an example, while automating a user account, creation of data might be needed from the Active Directory, as well as inputs from the person executing the Runbook. In this case, the Runbook can collect data from both parties and will make them available on the Data bus for later steps to use it.

In the following screenshot is an example of an activity and the extracted **Published Data** from a previous one to be used in this activity.

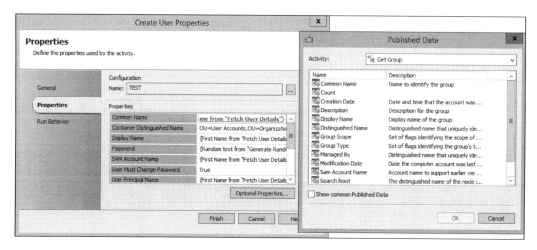

Understanding of how the **Data bus** and **Published Data** concepts work is very important, as you'll find yourself shifting data across activities many times during a Runbook design process. You'll get good at it once you start creating the Runbooks, but for now, let's address another very important part of the Runbook design process.

Global settings

In the Runbook Designer, you'll also notice a part called **Global Settings** on the **Connection** pane that contains in it **Counters**, **Variables**, and **Schedules**, as you can see in the screenshot that follows:

Global Settings can be set and used across Runbooks and each one has its own specialty and can bring convenience to your Runbook design process:

- **Counters**: These are entities that can be used to keep a count of anything. To add one, you just need to right-click on **Add Counter** under **Counters | New**, then specify the **Default value**, and you're done. They can be useful to keep track of how many times a certain thing was executed, or you can also use them as a flag to determine whether an event has occurred or not. Under **Utilities** on the **Activities** pane, you'll find the necessary activities to work with **Counters**.

- **Variables**: These are actually constant values as you won't be able to change the value of a variable from within a Runbook. We can use them to set a value that we use constantly across the Runbook in order to avoid having to set it multiple times per example. When you set a variable for a **Container Distinguished Name** on your Runbook, you can set it to something specific and then use only that variable across the Runbook. If you need to change that field, you only need to change the variable, which also allows you to edit the Runbook without even touching it. You can also use the option **Encrypted Variable** in order to protect the information within that variable that you're setting. This is useful when you're setting a password, for example.

- **Schedules**: These are preset date/time templates that can be used to allow or prevent the execution of an activity's path or an entire Runbook at a certain time or on a certain day.

Now that we've seen **Published Data** and the **Global Settings**, we're going to address how to use and manipulate that data as we wish.

Subscribe and Data Manipulation

There are two actions that can help on the manipulation of data on a Runbook; they are called **Subscribe** and **Data Manipulation**.

When you don't want to hardcode data, you can use the `Subscribe` function to fetch the data from a source dynamically. It can be either **Published Data** from a previous activity or a variable. In certain text boxes, you'll also find the possibility to subscribe a computer group; this is possible on activities that expect a computer name.

Let's say that we have a Runbook that creates user accounts in bulk from a SharePoint list that's populated by the HR department, and that in an activity, to add the user into an Active Directory Group, it needs to know that group in order to relate with the manager to later send the manager an e-mail saying that the account has been created successfully. In this case, we would use the `Subscribe` function from **Published Data** that would be captured from another activity and then feed into the **Add into AD Group** activity, so we wouldn't have to be writing the data again.

Now let's imagine that this field under SharePoint is not properly formatted, and that (for example) there's a drop-down list that has all the AD Groups listed, and that by selecting it, you get a friendly display name rather than a proper group name. When this happens, you can manipulate data through **Functions** that will allow you to properly consume data. As an example, let's take the group **Finance** from the SharePoint friendly name list (that's called by **Published Data**) and we know that this group is actually called **Fin** on our AD. To achieve this, we can perform the `[Left({Group Name from "SharePoint List Attributes"},3)]` function, which would translate the finance name and cut it down to **Fin**.

Looping

Loops are used to execute an activity multiple times depending on its condition. These conditions are called **Exit / Do Not Exit** conditions, and you can access them by right-clicking on the activity and selecting the option **Looping...** like in the following screenshot:

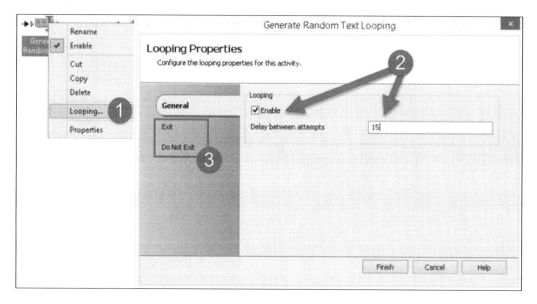

In order to get a proper loop in place, you'll need to check **Enable**, define the **Delay between attempts** (in seconds), and then configure the **Exit** condition, which will determine that the activity did what was expected, and the **Do Not Exit** condition, which will dictate why the activity needs to be repeated.

When you configure a loop, you'll see it in the Runbook as a smart link that links that activity to itself as in the following image:

In this case, let's imagine that the **Get User** activity fails to retrieve the user for some reason that will bring up a failure. As the exit of the activity is a failure, the activity will re-run after 15 seconds (that we've set in the loop settings) until it retrieves successfully.

Runbook Control

Before jumping into the Runbook design process, we're going to address some commonly used Runbook activities that will be handy when building your Runbooks, and you'll see yourself returning to them quite frequently.

For that, we'll talk about the **Runbook Control** activities under the **Activities** pane, where you can find four activities:

The four activities are explained in the following:

- **Initialize Data**: This activity is used to retrieve input directly from the user, or another Runbook, by injecting the data into the data bus to be used by the Runbook activities.

- **Return Data**: This will deliver data from a child Runbook to a parent Runbook. That's the only function it has.

- **Junction**: This activity can be used to merge different concurrent activities into one branch to follow a common activity. The junction will wait for all of them to complete before proceeding to the next activity down the flow. One very important piece of information about the converging multiple activities flowing into one branch is that only the published data from the selected activity is preserved, containing the data from all the activities preceding that one. This is controlled in **Details** under **Junction | Properties**, from which you select which of the activities data that connect to **Junction** should be kept.

- **Invoke Runbook**: This is used to call another Runbook and the Runbook that is using this activity is then called the parent Runbook or invoker. Consequently, the Runbook that gets called by this activity is referred to as the child Runbook or invoked. To the usage of this activity, we can also call it *nesting* as you're executing a Runbook invoked by another Runbook and you can continue doing so as necessary. Let's see what options we have when invoking a Runbook:

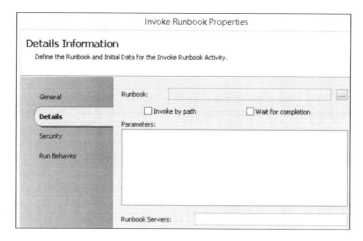

The **Invoke Runbook Properties** are explained in the following:

- The **Runbook (1)** option lets you decide which Runbook you want to invoke.

- The **Invoke by path (2)** option allows you to lock down the path in which the child Runbook should be. By default, this option is not enabled, and when you move the child Runbook, the parent Runbook gets automatically updated with the new location of the child Runbook. This option might be useful when you have a Runbook under development and then move it to production, where it's called by another parent Runbook, and you don't want the parent Runbook on development to call this child Runbook process as you might have already made changes into it that will reflect in production and create issues.

- The decision to activate **Wait for completion** (**3**) comes from the need to run the child Runbook sequentially (in case you check the option) or in parallel with the parent Runbook; if you decide to run it sequentially, you'll be able to retrieve data from the child Runbook into the parent Runbook, which won't be possible if you run them in parallel.

- In **Runbook Servers** (**4**), you can define where the child Runbook is allowed to run, and if you leave this unset, it will use the global definitions. Last but not least, the **Parameters** box allows you to pass specific values for input that the child Runbook needs to run; if the child Runbook has been configured to accept input, it will go up here.

Runbook design recommendations

In Orchestrator, we are not really forced or requested to follow standards or patterns in terms of Runbook design, in fact, the drawing area of the **Runbook Designer** is somehow *infinite*. Although there are no limits or restrictions, we need to impose them ourselves, and there are some best practices for Runbook design that we would like to call your attention to.

Every activity in Orchestrator (with the exception of the starting and ending point activities) has both an input and output side; most activities can actually have multiple inputs and outputs. If you use them properly, you'll find yourself using a left-to-right execution flow, but this only won't suffice to keep things organized.

A good way to keep your Runbook easily readable and organized is to divide it into three tiers. Let's take the next Runbook as an example, and we've already divided it into three zones so you'll understand the explanation.

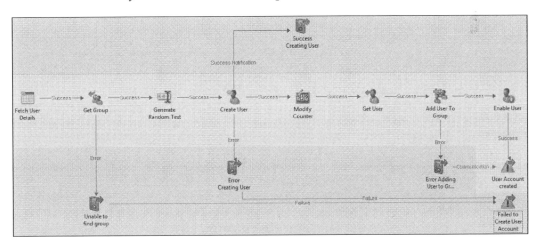

So, the first zone on top, the blue area, is called the **Notification** area, where we will place all the activities that trigger some sort of notification or that are used for auditing purposes. The middle (green) area is referred to as the Action or Main area that will be where all main Runbook activities will be placed. And finally, the red area, we'll refer to it as the **Error handling** zone, where we'll place all the mitigation or error reporting activities.

This is not a miraculous formula, but if you follow it, you'll handle your Runbook design and structure well, and if you run into a need of reviewing your Runbook, it will be much easier to make sense of all of it.

Also, don't forget that the use of link names, colors, and line thickness can also significantly improve the understanding of the Runbook flow and its design. Usually, we use the color green for successful conditions and red for errors, and other colors to distinguish when there are parallel executions, but that's a case of standards in your environment. The important thing is to have a standard to follow and to keep your design standard optimal and efficient, as this will be the key to how well your Orchestrator will perform.

Apart from the visual design, we also need to take into account a few other points, such as:

- **Gathering requirements**: Understanding and knowing what your Runbook is all about and gathering every piece of information that you need to know for the automation to be accomplished successfully.

- **Select activities**: Seeing beforehand which activity will fit for each point of the Runbook. Usually, a good flowchart, even made by hand on paper, will help you sketch your activities logically.

- **Keep standards**: Once you've accomplished the two tasks above, start putting the activity blocks into place and don't forget to keep a good naming convention for each one of them; also, pay good attention to the smart link color codes and label them.

- **Standardize and validate**: Don't forget the data manipulation or validation whenever necessary! It will be handy to transform the data and validate it accordingly to keep the Runbook running strictly as necessary and to make data useful.

- **Counters, Variables, and Schedules**: Whenever necessary, be sure to keep these at hand. Remember, the convenience of having a variable in place. You can change an entire Runbook execution by just changing the variable field. Take advantage of counters to keep a good track of the points that are executed on more complex Runbooks when you think that something's missing or when you just want to take a quick peek at the performance.

- **Exceptions**: Try to keep a good log and a track of all possible exceptions along your Runbook. These will help you fine-tune it and predict possible errors by the data input provided by users or even process output data that's not expected.

- **Split regular tasks into Runbooks**: To keep it simple, try to reduce your Runbook footprint or size by splitting it into smaller Runbooks that you can then call child Runbooks. Usually, a good idea is to make error handling, message logging, or file processing run in child Runbooks that you can then call from all other parent Runbooks that you design.

- **Verify, test and optimize**: Don't forget to test your Runbook and check if it does what's expected in a proper way and whether it's optimized to a good standard. Validate all the steps, try to induce some errors to see if the error activities are well triggered, and (why not) give it to someone else to test it for you! Usually, other people will find and test what we are not *expecting*.

Creation of a Runbook

You jumped right to this section of the book without knowing the details of a Runbook given on the previous point Runbook overview? You'll have to go back!

Let's start creating our first Runbook!

We're going to start by choosing a task to be automated, and to choose it, we will pick a day-to-day administrative task that actually takes long to accomplish, and it consumes time from your IT administrators or helpdesk. We'll try to get it automated in order to reduce the time consumption of man working hours. It only makes sense to automate something if the time invested to automate it doesn't go over the time otherwise taken by that task and the number of times (or frequency) with which the task is executed; otherwise, it's a total waste of time.

So, for the task in hand, we will automate free disk space management by archiving logs that exist on the server on a specific location.

Remember, this is the very first Runbook you'll do, and we haven't yet deployed any integration packs on Orchestrator, so we're looking at a bit of a reduced scope of action here.

Let's start!

Gathering requirements

Our mission here is simple. There's one server that has been identified as having issues with an application that does intensive logging, and our support colleagues complain that all they have to do is move the logs aside, compress them, place them in the archive, and check whether the disk space was released properly.

Although we're talking about one server, it's a business-critical application and the man-hours involved in this task rounds up to about 1 hour each day, and by the end of the week that's 5 hours consumed from a team member from the support team.

Activities selection

Ok, so on this Runbook, we're mainly talking about **Disk Space**, **Folder compression**, **File Archival**, and **Notification**. So, out of the box, the activities we will need will be the following:

- **Monitor Disk Space**
- **Move File**
- **Compress File**
- **Delete File**
- **Send Platform Event**

However, we'll end up using a bit more than this as we'll feel the need to improve our tracking of information across the activities and operations.

Flowcharts

OK, let's get our needs into a flowchart. To keep it a bit more visual, we've actually used the Orchestrator activity icons, but keep in mind that this is the very first *get your ideas into place* that you'll do, so a piece of paper and a pen is fine.

Here's the flowchart:

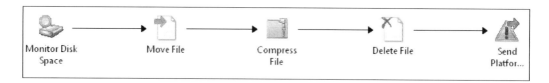

Though it might seem very basic in the flowchart, it would actually work if you implemented it this way. Let's go through it point by point. So, we start by **Monitor Disk Space** and verify that it has a certain percentage of disk space available, let's say 10 percent; if this 10 percent is breached, the activity will jump into the next one that will start **Move File** from the log's active folder into another folder (let's call it compress log folder) that we can work without *catching* a log that's in use; after this, it will compress the file we indicate, into a certain folder that can be the archive location; at this point, we can then delete the files that are in the compress log folder that we've just compressed, and finally, notify the admin.

Creating the Runbook

This is where we pick up the Runbook Designer where we left it to discuss the Runbook itself. We are now going to grab our requirement, our flowchart, and get them into place with all the necessary error treatment and auditing that we need.

Start by creating a new structure for this Runbook. Don't forget the organization. We would recommend a folder called **Files Management** under **Runbooks**, and underneath that, another folder called **Log Archiving**, and, underneath that, another folder called **v1.0** as in the screenshot you see here:

Right-click on that **v1.0** folder and navigate to **New | Runbook** on the menu and then **Check Out** the Runbook. This will open the **Runbook** for editing and lock it for you, avoiding someone else editing it at the same time.

You can right-click over the tab that has the Runbook name **New Runbook** and select **Rename** from the menu; and call it something more appropriate, such as **Log Automatic Archival**. It should then look like the following image:

Now let's get our activities into the Central pane. We'll start by dragging the **Monitor Disk Space** activity that's under **Monitoring**, and we'll then edit the **Monitor Disk Space Properties** of the activity and set it as seen in the following screenshot:

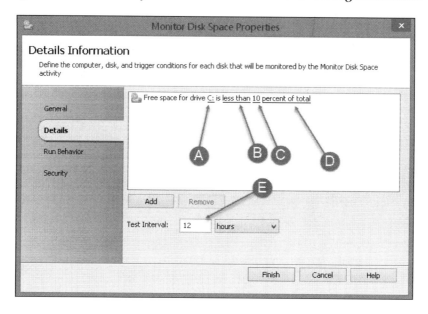

The settings here will be as follows:

- **A**: Select the drive that will be monitored by this activity, in this case **C:**.
- **B**: Choose the condition as **more than** or **less than**.
- C: Input the number.
- **D**: Select either **megabytes**, **percent of total**, or **gigabytes**.
- **E**: Set **Test Interval** that will give the time required to execute an activity. Here, we've chosen **12 hours** as the app is really demanding on log inputs.

Now we need to continue dragging and setting our activities in our Runbook. The physics are the same for each activity; you'll have to drag them and drop them into the Runbook; don't forget to keep a logic of left-to-right flow. For now its OK, but in the end, we'll *visually arrange* the activities into a proper standard Runbook.

Check out our **sweet new IT site** and be sure to enter the contest when you get there!

https://libertylife.sharepoint.com/sites/InformationTechnology
Link available in email

—Beth and Sandy

...ve File activity and configure it accordingly as

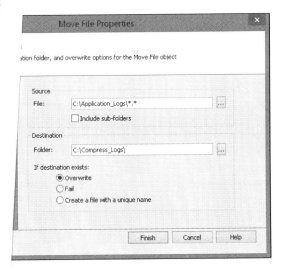

...the current `Application_Logs` folder into the working ... in the **Advanced** properties in this same activity, you can set whether you want to keep the same creation date or use the date when you moved. For this exercise, we're changing the setting to **Same as original**.

You can click on **Finish** and move on to the next one.

Now we'll get the **Compress File** activity from **File Management** into the Runbook and edit **Properties** as follows:

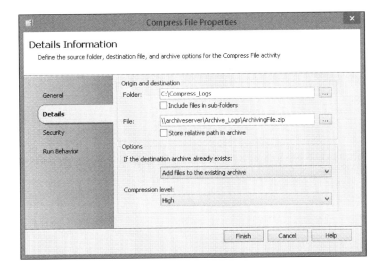

The options are almost self-explanatory.

We're going to compress everything that's inside the folder **Compress_Logs** into a log ZIP file in the location (and name) specified in **File**. As we're packing everything into one big log ZIP file, we will *append* the logs into the existing ZIP file. We'll soon see how to put a variable (such as the one in the following screenshot) into place here so we can use the date (and time) to create different ZIP files.

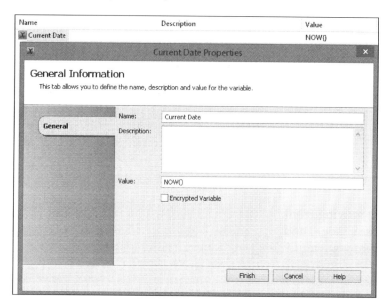

At this point, we have our logs compacted and moved into the archive, so it's time to clean the **Compress_Logs** folder. In order to achieve this, we use the **Delete File** activity and we set the properties as seen in the following screenshot:

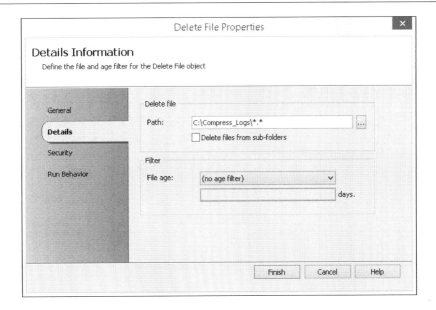

This way we'll leave the directory ready for another batch of logs to be compressed and sent into the archive.

Now, for the last step, we want to notify the Orchestrator console that it went fine and get a summary of what was done and what we can expect. For this, we'll use a **Send Platform Event** activity and we'll set it as seen in the next screenshot:

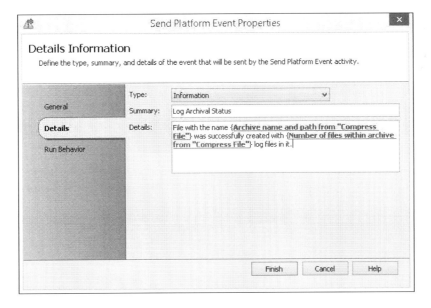

Don't forget that to get that **Published Data** you just need to right-click anywhere within the **Details** option box, navigate to **Subscribe | Published Data**, and then select the appropriate field you want.

In the end, your Runbook will look something like this:

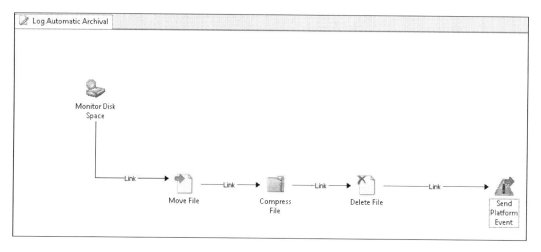

Notice that it's still checked out (as you can see in the sheet icon with the pen next to the name of the Runbook on top of the Central pane), also we've placed the activities like this because the **Monitoring Disk Space** activity is a monitoring/auditing activity; so to make a distinction, we kept it above to visually identify which tier it comes in to. Again, this is just a recommendation of mine and nothing written in stone, so you can organize yourself in another way that works better for you.

The Runbook will work as is, but we've seen a lot of good recommendations (such as auditing and error treatment), and those are not really there in this version (v 1.0) of the Runbook. This Runbook actually will stop if an error occurs because there's no other smart link apart from successful.

So, we invite you to evolve the Runbook into something more like this:

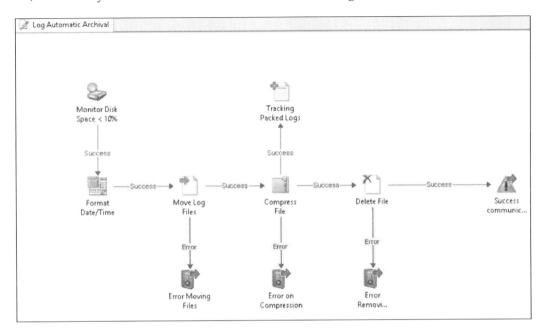

The Runbook has become a little bit more complex, but still simple enough for us to start developing and understanding the stages and tiers of the Runbook in this first phase.

We've added a few activities that are going to help us deal with possible failures in the core in case any of the errors are triggered, in order to know that an error (and which) was triggered in a user-friendly manner.

Also, we added another auditing activity that we will use to keep a track of a text file of the ZIP files created and the date, size, and number of log files within the ZIP file.

You might have noticed the **Format Date/Time** activity, which will actually format the output of the variable that we have concerning the date and time into a value that only concerns the date for our ZIP file.

In **Input Format**, please set the date in accordance with your system's regional definitions; for example, in Switzerland, we use **dd.MM.yyyy hh:mm**. If not set accordingly, this will fail.

Also notice the activity names and the smart link colors, they're visually important to understand and immediately decode how the Runbook is programmed to act.

Let's see what configurations we have in the additional steps.

In **Format Date/Time Properties**, we have the following options:

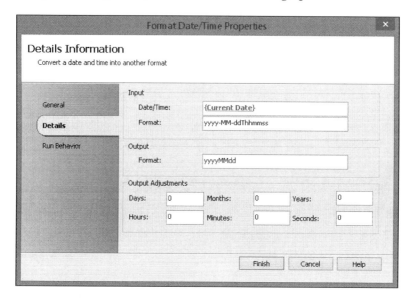

As you can see here, this will be the format adopted on the **Compress File** activity afterwards, which we will change in the filename to accommodate it appropriately. This is simply a step that provides the date in the format that we want to get our filename formatted to.

The **Compress File** activity will then be reconfigured in the **File:** property to something like this `\\archiveserver\Archive_Logs\{Format Result from "Format Date/Time"}.zip`.

The rest of the options in the activity can remain unchanged.

As previously mentioned, the **Tracking Packed Logs** activity will serve to keep a written record of date, ZIP filename, size, and number of log files in it. The activity chosen is actually **Append Line**, and that's all we're going to do, as you can see in the following properties:

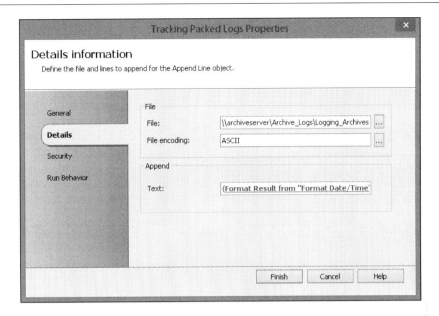

The settings here concern the text file to which we're adding the line, the type of **File encoding**, and which **Text** we want to add to it.

We've subscribed data as the text we're going to add into the file, and we've chosen the this information to keep in this record {Format Result from "Format Date/Time"} - File:{Archive name and path from "Compress File"} - Size:{Size of archive (bytes) from "Compress File"} bytes - Number of Logs:{Number of files within archive from "Compress File"}.

The sample output of this would be something like 20150325 - File:\\ archiveserver\Archive_Logs\20150325.zip - Size:1823747 bytes - Number of Logs:22.

Going to the error management level, we have three notifications (**Send Event Log Message**) included in our Runbook, so we can mitigate and give visibility to the console of any stop in the Runbook due to any of those critical core activities. If we hadn't included and configured these activities, you would still have an error in the Orchestrator console or in the **Logging** pane when the Runbook gets executed, but these activities will bring added value as they will make it more user-friendly and also include more information on why and where the error occurred.

Let's go through each one of them.

The very first one is under the **Move Log Files** activity, and we've called it **Error Moving Files**. Inside this activity, we can see the following properties:

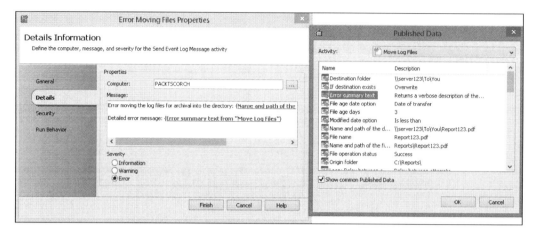

Now the preceding screenshot shows the properties that we've set for the message, the computer and the severity of the message. Also, we've set aside where you can find **Error summary text** from the activity. In order to see it from **Published Data**, you'll need to check the box **Show common Published Data**. After that, you select it, hit **OK** and **Finish**, and you're all set.

The other two error activities are similarly configured, but of course, the name of the activity and the **Published Data** source are not the same.

Here are the property settings for one of them:

- **Name**: Error on compression
- **Computer**: PACKTSCORCH
- **Message**: Error on compacting file: <Subscribed Data archive name and path from Compress File activity>Detailed error message: <Subscribed Data Error summary from Compress File activity>
- **Severity**: Error

The last one:

- **Name**: Error removing files
- **Computer**: PACKTSCORCH
- **Message**: Error on removing files Detailed error message: <Subscribed Data Error summary text from Delete File>
- **Severity**: Error

Now, in the **File Management** activities (**Move Log Files** and **Delete File** respectively in this Runbook) you'll need to set **Run Behavior** in order to avoid the other consecutive activities from running multiple times.

Why? Because when an activity in a Runbook runs, it runs one time for each item of data that the previous activity produced. In our case, when the **Move Log Files** activity runs, it will count one execution per log file it moves, and that information will be transformed into **Published Data** that you can use across the Runbook execution, making the **Compress Files** activity execute that same amount of times that the previous activity executed, and so on and so forth. These rows of data are extracted (let's say that it retrieved three files during the move files activity, so it will run three times for the next activity to run three times) one time for each row returned. This next activity does not have to subscribe to the data for this action to occur.

So to prevent this, you should set both activities mentioned here with the following settings:

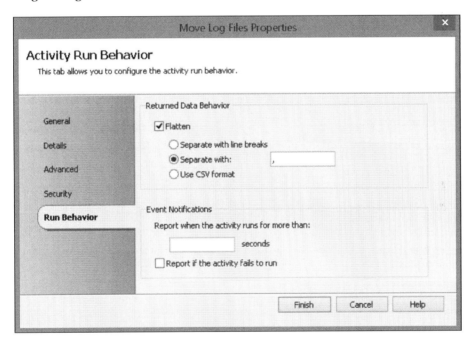

With this, we conclude this part of creating our first Runbook, now let's test it.

The Runbook Tester

To start the Runbook Tester, you just need to invoke it from the command button named **Runbook Tester** on **Commands Bar**. The Runbook has to be checked for it to be run in the tester; if you haven't checked it yet, the tester will request you to accept it, and do it for you.

The objective of the **Runbook Tester** is to help you verify that your Runbook is successfully configured and ready for deployment on production.

Once started, the **Runbook Tester** will show the following window:

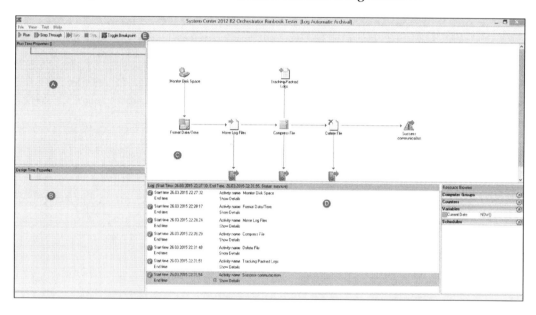

In this window you'll see:

- **A**: **Run Time** data that's executed. You'll see the data that each step retrieves when you use variables or published data. This will only show data when a breakpoint is hit.

- **B**: **Design Time Properties** is where all those properties we set in the activities are going to show up. Here, you'll be able to check and confirm that they are OK during the execution of the test.

- **C**: The Runbook design area allows you to see your Runbook design and the steps being executed.

- **D**: In the **Log** output, you can see details of each executed activity.

- E: The **Command** button area is where you can decide to run the Runbook without any stops, run it by clicking on the **Step Through** option (basically step-by-step where you'll have full control of the activities executed) and also the possibility of running it to create a **Breakpoint** to stop your Runbook at a designated moment.

Now, **Runbook Tester** runs locally on the machine you're executing **Runbook Designer** on, so pay attention to what settings you're making on it. In this case, **File Management** activities will execute locally on the machine that is running the Runbook Tester and therefore, in order to test, you have to have the expected data in place; otherwise, it will be impossible to test and verify.

Logging

When you execute the Runbook from the **Runbook Designer** or the **Orchestrator Console**, you will notice that logging occurs quite differently than it does when you do it from the Tester.

You can access the **Log** pane on the **Runbook Designer** and under the **Log** tab, you can retrieve information immediately as you see in the next screenshot, concerning the execution of the Runbook:

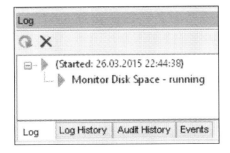

Once executed, you can view **Log History**, and that will have the details of each step executed on that Runbook; for example, if your Runbook has an activity that throws an exception, you'll be able to see in the **Runbook Details**, as in the following screenshot:

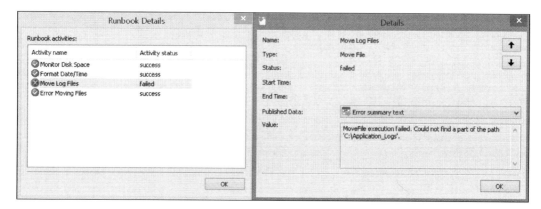

You'll also be able to view Runbooks that execute successfully and check **Published Data** that was handled by each activity.

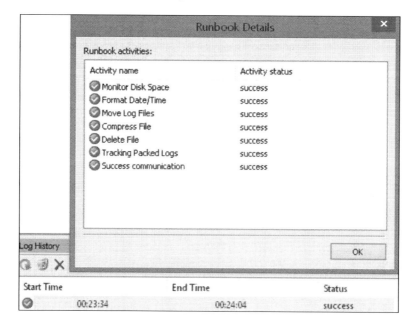

Summary

This concludes this chapter, where we saw the Runbook Designer and went deeper with Runbooks, seeing the detail of the Data bus and the published data and the importance of formatting it across the Runbook.

You're now able to identify activities (and connect them through smart links), and also mitigate some hidden issues with file management activities (such as execution of the repeated activities that follow a file management activity).

We also lightly addressed the check-in and check-out activities while going through the Runbook Designer and Runbook examples and their importance and the reasons we need to get a Runbook checked out.

You're now efficient in creating Runbooks and troubleshooting them, and you can create a Runbook while understanding the various components of it.

3
Orchestrator Integration Packs

Now that we've got good control of our Orchestrator architecture and know how to build and design new Runbooks, we can start looking around and figuring out that we actually can bring more automation to our processes and procedures, reducing their execution time and effort, but we see that we are missing a few activities that allow us to successfully accomplish those objectives.

This is where the Integration Packs come in by providing an additional layer of connectivity between Orchestrator and the other technologies that are available in our infrastructure.

In this chapter, we'll see what Integration Packs are and how to install them on our Orchestrator. Aside from that, we will see what configurations we need to pay attention to for the samples that we will address, and what they can essentially provide us.

One very important piece of information to retain is that there are third-party Integration Packs that are not free. When you do realize that, you'll need to assess and decide between the possible gains of buying that Integration Pack and/or try to deal with that automation in another way.

Deployment Manager

To start working with Integration Packs, we need to pass through the Deployment Manager. This is the part responsible for their deployment and can also be used in order to additionally deploy Runbook Designers as well as Runbook Servers. The following screenshot shows how the Deployment Manager looks when it is installed:

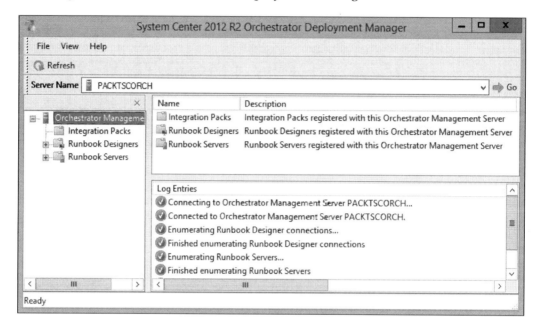

This console is available in the Management Server and you can see this in the **Log Entries** in the preceding screenshot.

Regarding the Integration Packs, our Deployment Manager will be responsible for their registration and deployment.

Let's move on to the Integration Packs. For now, we know what we need to know from the Deployment Manager.

Integration Packs

Microsoft makes a set of Integration Packs available to integrate Orchestrator with other technologies in your environment, allowing you to expand and create automation solutions for your needs.

Here's a list of Integration Packs that are available to you freely at Microsoft:

- System Center 2012 Integration Pack for Azure
- System Center 2012 Integration Pack for Active Directory
- System Center 2012 Integration Pack for Configuration Manager
- System Center 2012 Integration Pack for Data Protection Manager
- System Center 2012 Integration Pack for Exchange Admin
- System Center 2012 Integration Pack for Exchange User
- System Center 2012 Integration Pack for FTP
- System Center 2012 Integration Pack for Operations Manager
- System Center 2012 Integration Pack for REST
- System Center 2012 Integration Pack for Service Manager
- System Center 2012 Integration Pack for SharePoint
- System Center 2012 Integration Pack for Virtual Machine Manager

As expected, the other System Center family products are included in this Integration Pack's list. Most of them are self-explanatory about what technology they allow you to integrate with, but there's one that might not be so clear, that is, **Representational State Transfer** (**REST**); and therefore, we would like to give you a quick explanation about it.

The Integration Pack for REST has one activity (to invoke the REST service) that can make requests to the REST web services to get data or execute functions.

Through the course of this chapter, we will address only five Integration Packs that are usually the most commonly used in an infrastructure automation process. The chosen Integration Packs are as follows:

- System Center 2012 Integration Pack for Active Directory
- System Center 2012 Integration Pack for Configuration Manager
- System Center 2012 Integration Pack for Data Protection Manager
- System Center 2012 Integration Pack for Operations Manager
- System Center 2012 Integration Pack for Virtual Machine Manager

Let's get them into our Orchestrator!

In order to achieve this, download the package with the Integration Packs from the Microsoft website `http://www.microsoft.com/en-us/download/details.aspx?id=39622`.

Once you have it, execute the `System_Center_2012_R2_Integration_Packs.exe` file, and on the **Choose Directory For Extracted Files** screen, select a directory into which you have permissions to access and unpack your Integration Packs.

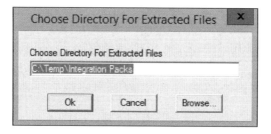

Once finished, you'll see a screen confirming that the extraction completed, and you'll just have to press **OK**.

In the end, in the directory you've selected you will see the following:

Name	Date modified	Type	Size
attributions.txt	17/09/2013 16:13	Text Document	2 KB
SC2012R2_Integration_Pack_for_Azure.oip	17/09/2013 16:52	OIP File	880 KB
SC2012R2_Integration_Pack_for_Configuration_Manager.oip	14/03/2014 17:13	OIP File	858 KB
SC2012R2_Integration_Pack_for_Data_Protection_Manager.oip	17/09/2013 16:52	OIP File	707 KB
SC2012R2_Integration_Pack_for_Operations_Manager.oip	14/03/2014 17:13	OIP File	447 KB
SC2012R2_Integration_Pack_for_REST.oip	14/03/2014 17:13	OIP File	623 KB
SC2012R2_Integration_Pack_for_Service_Manager.oip	17/09/2013 16:52	OIP File	1 523 KB
SC2012R2_Integration_Pack_for_Virtual_Machine_Manager.oip	17/09/2013 16:52	OIP File	988 KB
System_Center_2012_R2_Integration_Pack_for_ActiveDirectory.oip	17/09/2013 16:23	OIP File	874 KB
System_Center_2012_R2_Integration_Pack_for_ExchangeAdmin.oip	14/03/2014 13:42	OIP File	703 KB
System_Center_2012_R2_Integration_Pack_for_ExchangeUser.oip	17/09/2013 16:26	OIP File	937 KB
System_Center_2012_R2_Integration_Pack_for_FTP.oip	17/09/2013 16:29	OIP File	1 047 KB
System_Center_2012_R2_Integration_Pack_for_SharePoint.oip	15/03/2014 10:38	OIP File	1 500 KB

Once you have all this prepared, you can proceed with the next steps of registering the Integration Packs and deploying them into the Runbook Designer. We'll also see what activities they bring and how to troubleshoot any issues arising during the registration or deployment of the Integration Packs.

Registering Integration Packs

We'll start by registering one Integration Pack into Orchestrator through the Deployment Manager, and then we'll see how to register a bunch of them at the same time.

To start the integration process, open the **Deployment Manager** console and select **Integration Packs**, which at this moment should be empty (don't worry, we're going to fill that up quickly). Right-click on it and you'll see two options, as in the following screenshot:

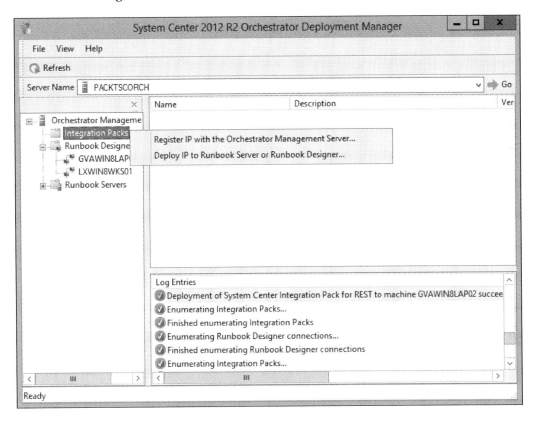

These two options are the initial options that you'll have available to work with Integration Packs. Right now, we need **Register IP with the Orchestrator Management Server...** just to get the Integration Pack in to our inventory so we can use it to deploy into the Runbook Server or Designer, depending on what we're looking for.

So, after pressing the option to register **Integration Pack** into Orchestrator, you'll see the first screen for the **Integration Pack Registration Wizard**. That will explain what you're about to experience and what will be expected from your side in just a few sentences.

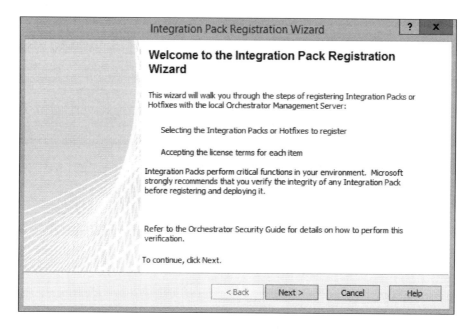

Press **Next** and we'll get into the **Integration Pack or Hotfix Selection** screen, where we will add and select the Integration Pack that we want. For this example, we'll register the Active Directory Integration Pack with the name **System_Center_2012_R2_Integration_Pack_for_ActiveDirectory.oip**.

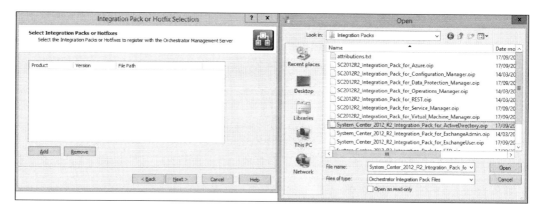

Once you press **Open**, you'll see the Integration Pack in the **Integration Pack or Hotfix Selection** screen, along with the version and the path from which you're importing the file.

Then you should press **Next** and you'll be presented the **Completing Integration Pack Registration Wizard** screen, which is basically a summary of what you're about to register into your Management Server.

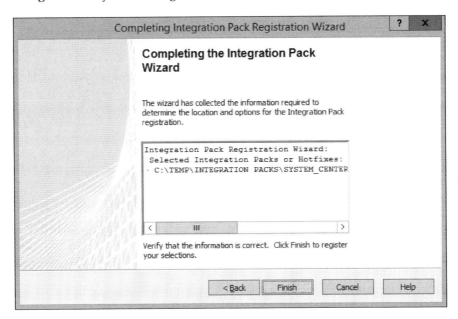

Press **Finish**, then read and accept the license terms displayed, and you'll be back into the Deployment Manager.

Then go into **Integration Packs** and you'll see your newly-arrived Integration Pack registered there. In the **Log Entries** section, you will see the output of that registration and if it was successful or not, just like in the next screen:

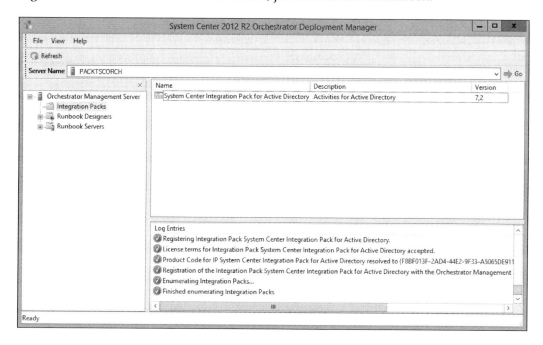

This concludes a single Integration Pack registration process.

Now, in the beginning of your work with Orchestrator, you'll have a few Integration Packs to register into your newly installed Orchestrator architecture, and you might be wondering if you'll need to register them one by one. The answer is: No! You can register multiple Integration Packs at the same time by selecting all of them. Let's see how that's done.

We start the same way as we start for a single registration process:

1. Right-click on **Integration Packs**.
2. On the wizard's first page, click on **Next**.

3. Now click on **Add**, and in the explorer window, select your Integration Pack and click on **OK**. Repeat this process for the next Integration Pack, and in the end you should have something like this:

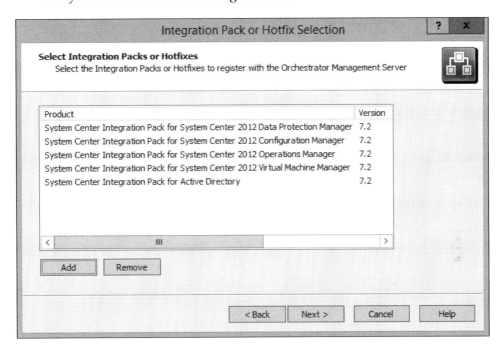

4. Press **Next** and review the completion screen, and then press **Finish**.

5. The license screen will show up for each Integration Pack. You need to accept the license terms so the Integration Pack gets installed.

That's it. You'll then see all the Integration Packs you selected installed and available for deployment to the Runbook Servers and Runbook Designers.

Similar to the single registration process, you'll have the information concerning the Integration Pack's registration available on the log entries.

For now, all you have is the Integration Packs available in your Management Server. Now we need to deploy them so we can see the new categories and activities and use them in our Runbooks.

Deploying Integration Packs

Once your Integration Packs have been registered, you'll need to deploy them into the Runbook Servers and Runbook Designers that need them. This can be achieved through the Deployment Manager, and it basically consists of an MSI that's transferred into the machine that has the Runbook Designer and/or Runbook Server, and it's then executed and installed accordingly to allow you to have access to its activities and integrate them into your Runbook.

We'll start by deploying the Integration Packs first into the Runbook Server and then to the Runbook Designers and see all the steps it takes to accomplish this task.

To start the process, we go to the **Integration Packs** folder on our **Deployment Manager**, right-click on one of the Integration Packs, and select the option **Deploy IP to Runbook Server or Runbook Designer...** like in the following screenshot:

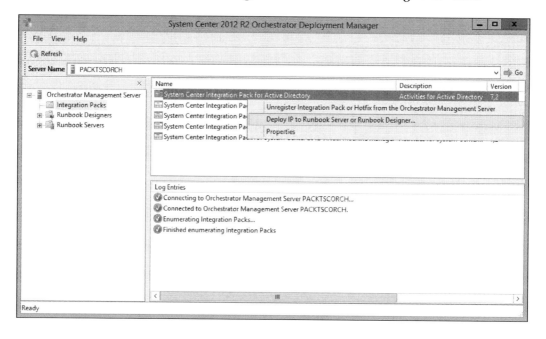

This will start **Deployment Wizard** that will start by showing us the welcome screen. You can disable this screen for future deployments by selecting the checkbox **Skip this welcome page in the future**. The next screenshot shows an example of this screen:

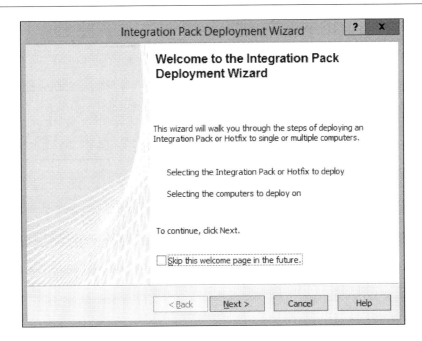

After clicking on **Next**, you'll arrive to the selection screen for the Integration Pack that you wish to deploy. In our case, we'll select all the Integration Packs available in our Management Server because we're deploying them initially into the Runbook Server, as you can see in the next screenshot:

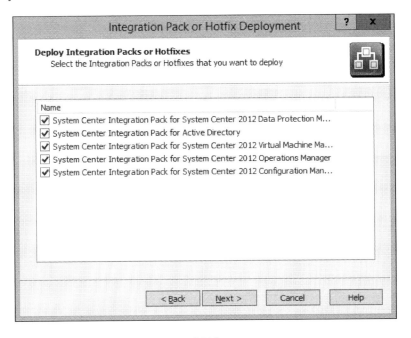

The possibility of selecting different Integration Packs to be deployed to Runbook Designers is (for example) the fact that you might have someone working with Active Directory and will only need to have Active Directory-related activities in his Runbook Designer.

Once we have selected the Integration Packs that we wish to deploy to our Runbook Server (in this case), we'll hit **Next** and arrive at the **Computer Selection** screen where we will add our Runbook Server name (in our case, it is just one; if you have multiple, you can add them here and you can deploy the Integration Packs to multiple Runbook Servers at same time).

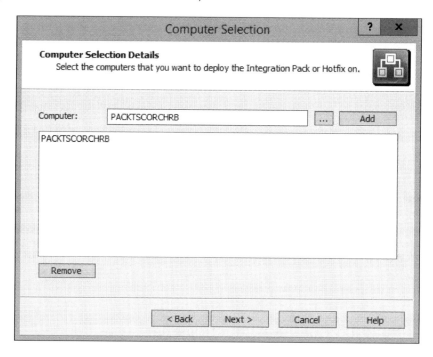

Once you have all the servers added to the **Computer Selection** screen, you can proceed with **Next**, and you'll then arrive at the **Installation Options** screen, where you can schedule an installation for a later time or leave the option unselected to install immediately, and you can also request for the Runbooks to be stopped before installing the Integration Packs.

These are very useful options if you're deploying a new Integration Pack into an production environment that has a high demand for Runbooks and can't have any amount of downtime. In these environments, usually there's a maintenance window that you can use by setting these options:

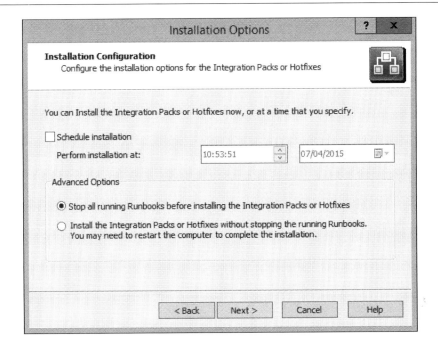

After setting these options and hitting **Next**, you'll have the summary of the actions to be performed, and you can then verify whether everything's OK. In the end, press **Finish**, and the installation will move on.

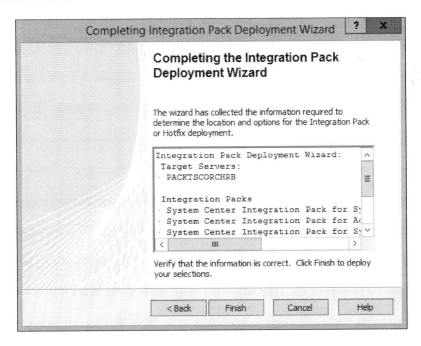

Once the action is complete, you can go to **Runbook Servers** and select the Runbook server to which you've deployed the Integration Packs, and you can then verify that they're installed. You can also verify the versions and the **Product Code** associated to it.

You can also verify the installation in **Log Entries** as usual, as you'll see in the following screenshot:

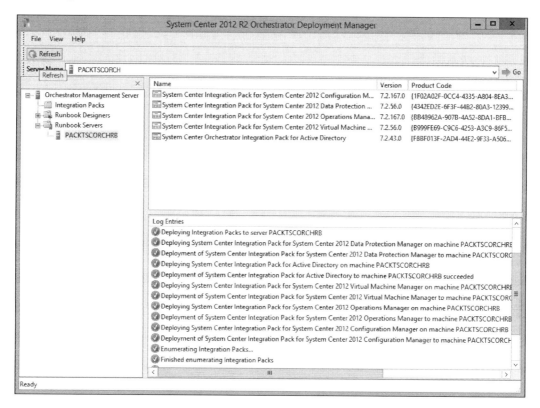

To deploy the Integration Packs to the Runbook Designer (or multiple Runbook Designers), the process is basically the same; the only change is the name of the computer to which you're deploying in the **Computer Selection** screen.

At any time, you can see which computers have the Runbook Designer registered with the Management Server by browsing into the Runbook Designers in the Deployment Manager, as in the following screenshot:

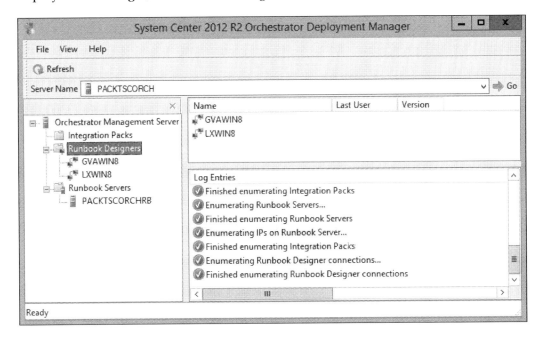

Once you've deployed your Integration Packs into the Runbook Designers, you can confirm the good deployment by selecting the Runbook Designer machine and checking the Integration Packs, versions, and product codes installed. You can also verify the log entries.

 Don't forget that the account with which you're running the Deployment Manager has to have permissions on the machines into which you're deploying the Integration Packs; otherwise, the installation will fail. Also ensure that the firewall ports are opened.

Now that you have the Integration Packs successfully deployed in the Runbook Designers, you can see the new categories and activities in the console:

Within these new categories, you'll find new activities that will expand and improve the integration between your Runbooks and the technologies involved.

Let's take the example of the **Active Directory** category. Here are the activities you'll see:

The list of activities continues to the right (there's the browsing bar at the bottom), but this is a sample of the new activities you'll see in your Runbook Designer, and that will help you in the creation process.

Configuring the new categories

Now, at this stage, before starting to use the new activities available, we need to configure the base options for them.

Active Directory

We'll take **Active Directory** as a sample for now. You'll need to set the domain configuration in order to advance and be able to use it during the execution of your Runbooks and in the activities you use. This is referred to as a connection, which is a reusable link between Orchestrator and as many Active Directory Domain Controllers as you need or are necessary.

In order to configure this prerequisite, you'll need to navigate to **Options | Active Directory** on your Runbook Designer bar menu that will present you the following screen:

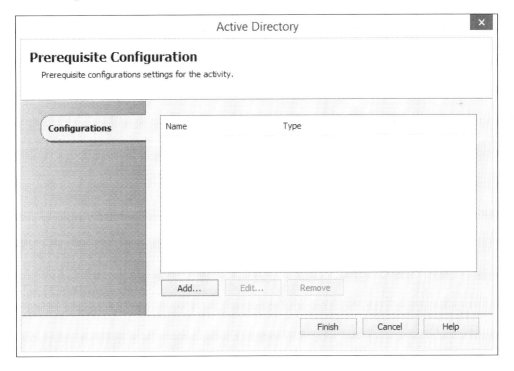

You then need to add a new Active Directory connection and configure it accordingly, as the following screenshot suggests:

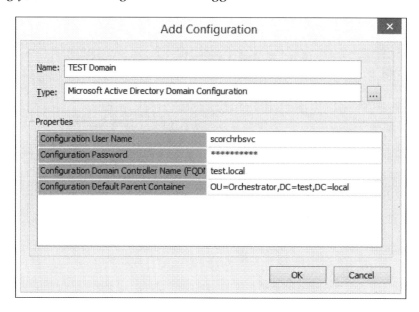

A brief explanation of these settings is as follows:

- **Name**: We will suggest something that identifies the domain to which this connection belongs, like the example that you see in the preceding screenshot.

- **Type**: This is typically **Microsoft Active Directory Domain Configuration**, and there isn't much to be added here.

- **Configuration User Name**: This user account must have the authority to perform the actions in any Runbook where the connection is used.

- **Configuration Password**: This is the password for the user account mentioned previously.

- **Configuration Domain Controller Name (FQDN)**: You can use either the domain or the domain controller name here.

- **Configuration Default Parent Container**: Type the distinguished name for an organizational unit or a common name. This default will be used when an activity such as create user or create computer does not specify the container distinguished name.

A good practice will be to create a specific organizational unit under your Active Directory structure, where you'll give permissions to the account specified here (We've used the Runbook Service account, though you might prefer to use another account due to your environment's security specifications) to create objects.

Usually, this default container should not be used, as you'll configure everything nicely in the Runbooks, either directly or by setting up a variable.

Once you have set things accordingly for your environment, click on **OK** and then on **Finish**.

System Center Configuration Manager

Now let's take another example of the configuration of the new categories, and for this one, we'll use **System Center Configuration Manager**. Accessing it takes the same process as accessing the Active Directory configuration seen earlier; so on the menu bar, go to **Options | SC 2012 Configuration Manager**, and there you'll find the following screen:

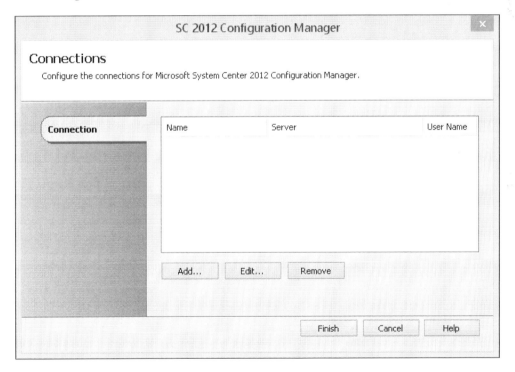

You'll then press **Add...** and configure the new **Connection Entry** for your SCCM server.

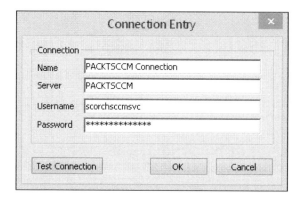

Let's detail these options for a better understanding:

- **Name**: This is the name of the connection for your reference. Let's say, SERVERNAME Connection.

- **Server**: This is your SCCM Server name; here, you can use the hostname (NetBIOS) or the FQDN.

- **Username**: Here, you set the credentials that Orchestrator will use to connect to the Configuration Manager Site Server. Note that the username includes the domain name, for example, DOMAIN\scorchsccmsvc.

- **Password**: This is the password for the username account you're using.

You can then test the connection with the **Test Connection** button that should return a **Successfully Connected** message, and you can then press **OK** to exit.

Press **OK** on the **Connection Entry** window, and then **Finish** on the **SC 2012 Configuration Manager** window.

System Center Operations Manager

All that is missing now is the **SC 2012 Operations Manager**, so we can close this chapter around the Integration Packs, their deployment, and configurations.

This Integration Pack configuration is mostly the same as the **System Center Configuration Manager**, where you'll be pointing to a server with credentials that have access and permissions to execute the necessary tasks and that's it.

So, to configure it, you'll need to go to the menu bar on **Options | SC 2012 Operations Manager**, press **Add...**, and the following window will be displayed:

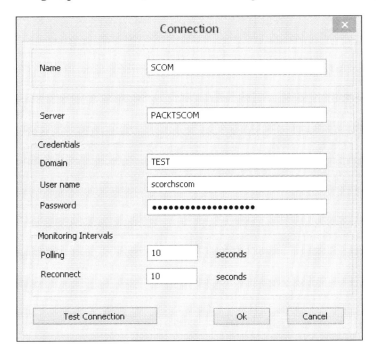

These options are very straightforward and have the same explanation as the previous point. The **Monitoring Intervals** field might be something you'll like to change according to your infrastructure and your needs, so you don't overload the entire SCOM with multiple queries.

For now, all we needed to have in order to achieve and accomplish these connections is an account with enough access and firewall ports open to achieve this. This will also be the case for other Integration Packs such as **SC 2012 Service Manager**, but for some Integration Packs such as **SC 2012 Data Protection Manager** and **SC 2012 Virtual Machine Manager**, you'll have to check other components before advancing.

System Center Virtual Machine Manager

We'll use **SC 2012 Virtual Machine Manager** as an example of what needs to be verified before moving forward.

The **Virtual Machine Manager Integration Pack** uses Windows PowerShell Remoting to make information pass between Orchestrator Runbook server and the Virtual Machine Manager Administration console. Windows PowerShell Remoting relies on **Windows Remote Management (WinRM)** to establish the connection between both systems. You'll need to perform the following tasks before you can configure the Virtual Machine Manager connection in the Runbook Designer.

Verify that you at least have Windows PowerShell 2.0 installed on the Virtual Machine Manager computer that runs the administration console.

In order to do this, perform the following steps:

1. Open the **Registry** editor.
2. Expand the `HKEY_LOCAL_MACHINE\SOFTWARE\Microsoft\PowerShell\1\PowerShellEngine` subkey.
3. Confirm that the value of the runtime version entry begins with a value above v2.0.
4. If this value begins with 1.0 or is not present, you'll need to install Windows PowerShell 2.0 or later. Check the Web on how to do so.

Usually, you should be fine with the Windows PowerShell version installed on your computer, as we imagine you're going to be using Windows Server 2012 R2 or Windows 8.1 in your environment, so with those two OS's, you'll have the latest version of Windows PowerShell and this won't be an issue.

If that's not the case, or you're running older OS versions, we strongly encourage you to verify these parameters.

WinRM requires you to specify the name of any host computers that you're going to connect to. This will enhance Orchestrator Runbook Server security by ensuring that it is only connecting to the expected computer running the Virtual Machine Manager Administration Console. This must be configured on both machines involved.

To confirm that WinRM is properly set, perform the following steps:

1. Open the `gpedit.msc` console.
2. Under **Local Computer Policy**, expand **Computer Configuration**, then **Administrative Templates**, and finally **Windows Components**.

3. Verify that Windows Remote Management (WinRM) is listed.

   If this is not listed, you'll need to install WinRM 2.0.

If you've found WinRM to be well-presented and configured, in order to achieve what has been listed previously, you'll need to do the following:

1. On the Orchestrator Runbook Server, open the `gpedit.msc` console.

2. Under **Local Computer Policy**, expand **Computer Configuration**, then **Administrative Templates**, then **Windows Components**, then **Windows Remote Management**, and then select **WinRM Client**.

3. Double-click on **Trusted Hosts**.

4. In the **Trusted Hosts** dialog box, select **Enabled**.

5. Add the name or the IP address of the computer running the **Virtual Machine Manager Administration Console** to the **TrustedHostsList** and click on **OK**.

Here's a sample of this configuration:

After this, set the PowerShell execution policy to `RemoteSigned` and you're good to go.

Now let's set the **SC 2012 Virtual Machine Manager** connection.

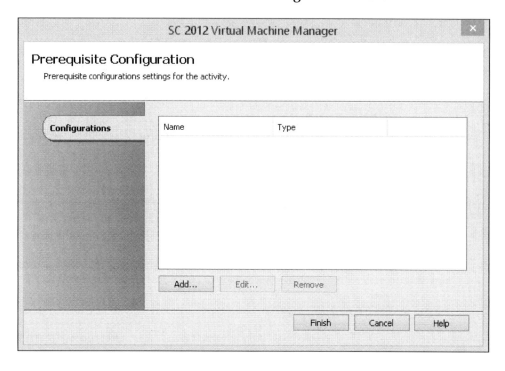

Once you click on **Add...**, you'll be presented with the **Add Configuration** screen, where you'll have to set the following options:

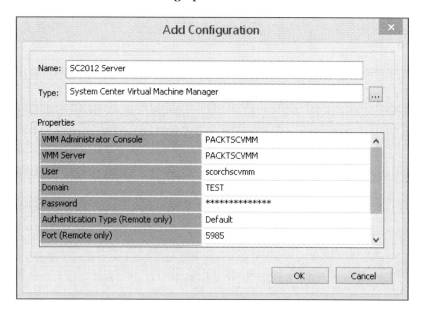

These settings are presented in depth here:

- **VMM Administration Console**: This is the name or IP Address of the computer running the Virtual Machine Manager Administration Console.

- **VMM Server**: This is the name of the Virtual Machine Manager Server that the action will be performed on. You can use a localhost if the Virtual Machine Manager Administration Console is installed on the VMM Server.

- **User**: This is the username account used to access the Virtual Machine Manager Administration Console. This account should have permissions to perform the actions requested by the activities. If you don't specify an account here, the Runbook Service Account will be used, so if that account has permissions, you don't need to set anything here.

- **Password**: This is the password for the username account used.

- **Authentication Type (Remote only)**: This is the type of authentication to use. This is only required if the Runbook Server and Virtual Machine Manager Administration Console are installed on different computers. The authentication method that you choose must be enabled in WinRM. You can enable the authentication methods using the local group policy editor.

- **Port (Remote only)**: This is the port used for PowerShell remoting between the Orchestrator Runbook Server and the computer with the Virtual Machine Manager Administration Console. This is only required if the Runbook Server and Virtual Machine Manager Administration Console are installed on different computers.

- **Use SSL (Remote only)**: This specifies whether SSL should be used for the connection. This is only required if the Runbook Server and Virtual Machine Manager Administration Console are installed on different computers.

- **Cache Session Timeout (min.)**: This is the number of minutes before the session times out from lack of activity and needs to reconnect.

Once you finish configuring it, you can press **OK** and then **Finish** to close the configuration.

After a good analysis of all the requirements and access needs mentioned previously, one good way to go is to have the Virtual Machine Manager Administration Console installed locally on your Runbook Servers so you can avoid the complexity of having to set all the fields seen above, and improve the usability of the console by executing everything locally.

System Center Data Protection Manager

The same type of pre requisites check applies to the **SC 2012 Data Protection Manager** Integration Pack, as this will use PowerShell Remoting to execute the necessary tasks triggered by the activities.

So, after checking the pre requisites as explained in the previous point concerning the System Center Virtual Machine Manager, you can execute the following steps to configure the connection.

Go to **Options | SC 2012 Data Protection Manager**, and in the first screen, click on **Add...** to open the **Add Configuration** screen, as you can see in the following screenshot:

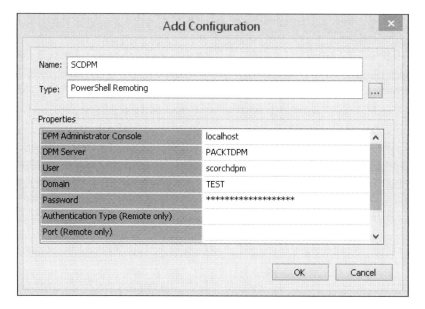

So, as you can see, the settings are pretty much the same as in SC 2012 Virtual Machine Manager Connection, although the **Type** field is different.

Once again, if you have the console installed locally, you won't need to be configuring the **Remote only** fields.

Summary

This concludes the third chapter concerning the Integration Packs. At this point, you'll be able to register, deploy, and configure the main Integration Packs offered by Microsoft, which we will use through this book and reference in Runbooks.

You're now also aware of how to verify the good registration and deployment of an Integration Pack, and you can safely provide more integration with your environment.

You can also troubleshoot and find the necessary information to mitigate issues with either registration of the Integration Packs in the Management Server, or the deployment to Runbook Servers and Runbook Designers.

4
Extending Orchestrator

In this chapter, we'll address all the connection points that allow us to extend Orchestrator and its usability. Orchestrator is a very flexible tool that we've deployed and explored until now in a very limited scope; now we're going to expand that scope with the aid of components that allow us to extend its connectivity towards access to it by users or other IT administrators that need to execute Runbooks, verify the good execution of their Runbooks, or even check the jobs executed.

Over and above this, we will see how we can offer internal developers the possibility to integrate with Orchestrator, allowing a much richer, more extended, and more open Orchestrator to help in our environment.

We will cover the following topics in this chapter:

- Overview of the Orchestration console and how the rights and delegations work
- Review of the Deployment Manager
- Installation of the Orchestrator Integration Toolkit and how to use it
- Why and how to use the web service and what it can be useful for

An overview of the Orchestration console

We are going to start by checking what the Orchestration console is, how it is organized, and what operations can be triggered from it.

Let's start by looking at it and analyzing its parts.

If you would like to follow this analysis in your environment with your recently installed Orchestrator architecture, you can do it by opening a browser (remember you'll need Silverlight installed) and typing the address of the server that hosts the Orchestration console and the port you've defined during the setup. In our example of a multiple server deployment set in *Chapter 1, Configuring and Deploying Orchestrator 2012 R2*, we'll use `http://packtscorchw:82`, as you can see in the following screenshot:

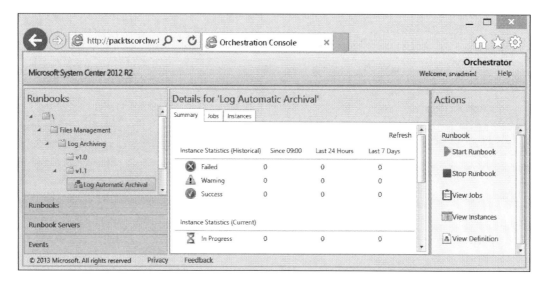

In **Orchestration Console**, you can perform the following operations:

- View a list of **Runbooks** and **Runbook Servers**
- View the current status and history of the Runbook's execution
- View high-level definition of Runbooks
- **Start** and **Stop** Runbooks
- View events that **Runbook Servers** and **Management Servers** can create

Let's position ourselves on the console concerning these points we've just listed.

On the left side of the console, you'll have a navigation pane from where you can access **Runbooks**, **Runbook Servers**, and **Events**.

The Runbook folders and Runbooks you'll see here are the ones you have set permissions for in the Runbook Designer. If you don't have permissions on some folders or Runbooks, you won't see them here.

 Keep this in mind for when you give permissions to a certain user over a specific Runbook and someone else says that he doesn't have access to that Runbook; this will be a very important thing to remember.

On the right side, you can trigger actions that will change to match the part you're navigating in at that moment. For instance, at the Runbooks, you'll have the ability to:

- **Start** and **Stop** Runbooks
- **View Jobs**
- **View Instances**
- **View Definition**

The **Start** and **Stop** Runbook actions, as the name suggests, allow you to start the Runbook you've selected and this will trigger a job that you can see and follow through the **View Jobs**.

The **View Jobs** Runbook will detail the completion status when you have a Runbook selected; when it's a folder, it will list the jobs created for all Runbooks in that folder and their completion status. A job is a request for a Runbook Server to run a Runbook and is created every time a Runbook receives a request to run. If the executed Runbook starts with a monitoring activity, it creates a job that runs continuously until that Runbook is stopped. In this case, the status of that job is an hourglass that indicates the job is still running.

Connected to the jobs and Runbooks are the instances. **View Instances** Runbook lists the instances that have been created on the Runbook Server and their completion status. An instance is a running copy of a Runbook and is created each time that Runbook runs. If the Runbook starts with a monitoring activity, it will create an instance that continues to run until the monitoring activity is completed and will then move to the next one. As with the jobs, here you'll also see an hourglass in case the Runbook starts with a monitoring activity.

While the instance is running, the real-time execution of it will also be visible as the activities are executed.

Now, continue to focus on the right pane. As stated previously, the Runbook Server workspace changes the **Actions** pane into a tad bit different selection of options, as you can see in the following screenshot:

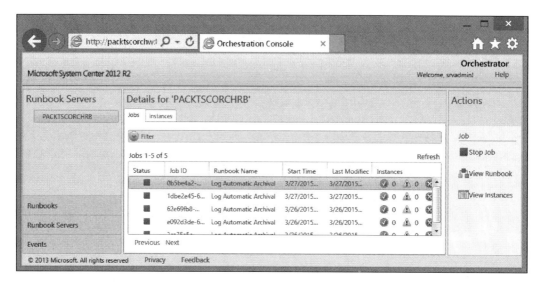

In the case of the **Runbook Servers** workspace, you will be able to list **Jobs** and **Instances** and their current status.

You'll notice that in the central pane, you have tabs in either of the workspaces you select. These allow you to quickly move between **Summary**, **Jobs**, and **Instances**.

Last but not least, the **Events** workspace that will let us see the events from the **Management Server** and all **Runbook Servers**.

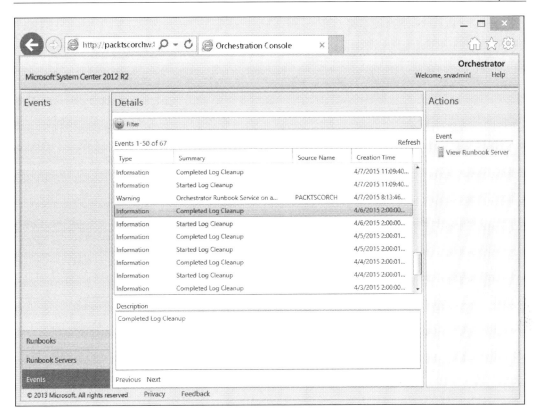

Now, regarding **View Definition**, when you're going through a Runbook in **Orchestration Console**, this will allow you to see the Runbook design but not alter it; for that, you have to use the Runbook Designer.

Also, you have to keep in mind the difference between these two subtools of Orchestrator, that is, **Orchestration Console** and **Runbook Designer**. Although the functions of the Orchestration console are a subset of the ones from the Runbook Designer, they have a totally different target usage.

The Runbook Designer is to be used during the design and testing of the Runbook, while the Orchestration console is used to view and execute the Runbooks in production. The Runbook Designer has to be installed locally into the computer of the person developing the Runbook; the Orchestration console can be run from any computer with a compatible browser.

Deployment Manager

We've already addressed this component of Orchestrator in *Chapter 3, Orchestrator Integration Packs*, but at that point, we were targeting only the Integration Packs deployment.

So far, we've addressed the Integration Packs registration and deployment against our Runbook Servers and Runbook Designers to get the activities that will allow us to integrate with other systems in our datacenter.

Now, the Deployment Manager can also help you deploy more from Orchestrator, more specifically:

- Deploy Runbook Servers remotely from the Management Server, as long as you have the permissions to do so
- Deploy the Runbook Designer remotely as well, allowing you to closely control the access and permissions given to the people that develop Runbooks

A few things to keep in mind before starting the deployment of new Runbook Servers through the Deployment Manager or even Runbook Designers are as follows:

- Don't forget to get the requirements installed properly beforehand, otherwise you will find some that will fail to install (for example, System Center Configuration Manager 2012 and System Center Data Protection Manager 2012 Integrations simply won't deploy).
- Permissions to install and/or deploy the component that you're trying to deploy. The account you're using should have permissions to carry on with the operation.

So, here's the procedure to deploy a Runbook Server through the Deployment Manager:

1. Deploy the machine OS that will be hosting the service (don't forget the prerequisites).

2. Configure your account to have the proper permissions to install and manage that server.

3. Get that server up to date in terms of updates.

4. Open **Deployment Manager** from your **Management Server** and right-click on **Runbook Servers** and select **Deploy new Runbook Server**.

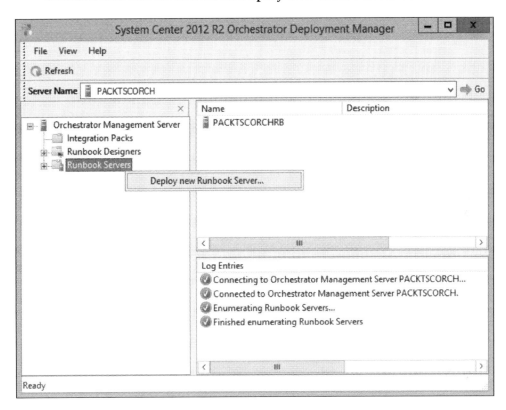

5. This will open the welcome screen of the **Runbook Server Deployment** wizard, where you can tick the checkbox to skip this page in the future and push **Next**.

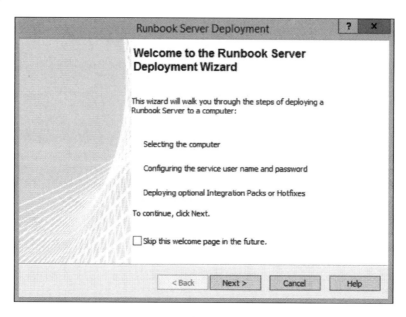

6. You'll then have to specify the server that will get the Runbook Server component deployed, and the service account for the **Runbook Server Service Account**, and then push **Next**.

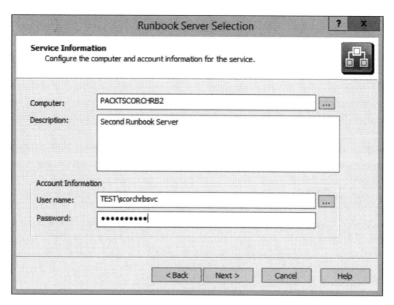

7. We will then get into the part of selecting which **Integration Pack or Hotfix Deployment** gets deployed along into this server. This allows us to save time and avoid having to come back to this server at a later stage and deploy the Integration Packs *by hand*. As we're configuring a second Runbook Server for general use, we'll deploy all the Integration Packs into it. Push **Next**.

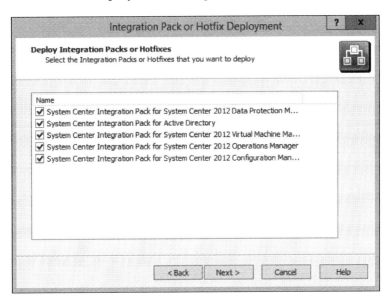

8. Then, we'll arrive at **Completing Runbook Server Deployment**, where we'll review our settings and press **Finish** to get everything installed.

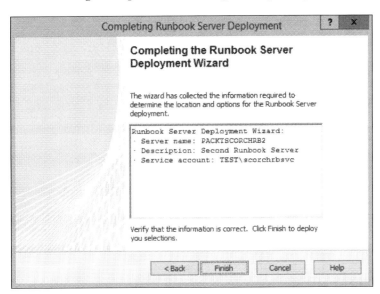

9. After the conclusion of the process, you can browse back to the Runbook Servers, where you'll see your freshly installed Runbook Server, and in **Log Entries** you can see the status of each task and whether they concluded successfully or whether there was any error, just like in the following screenshot:

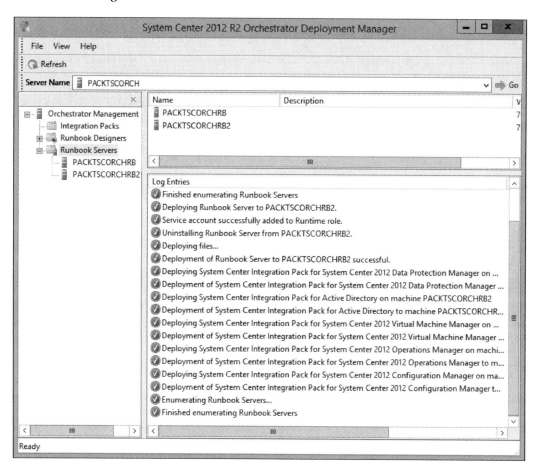

10. If, by any chance, for instance, you don't install the prerequisites on the server where you're going to deploy the Runbook Server component, you might have a **Log Entries** window a bit like this:

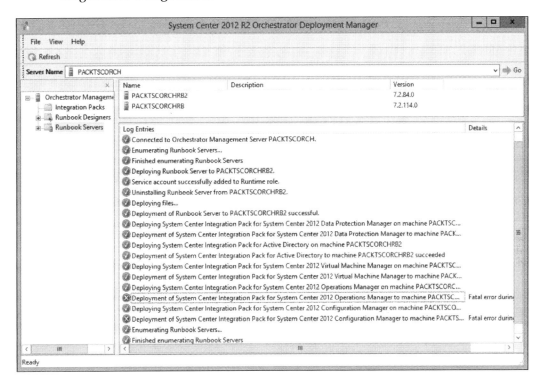

As we can see in the preceding screenshot, there were only two Integration Packs that didn't get installed, that's only because they need .NET Framework 3.5 SP1 installed in order to be deployed; if you don't have the .NET 3.5 SP1 installed, the installation will fail.

You can also deploy the .NET 3.5 SP1 after the installation of the Runbook Server in this case, but as a good practice, we should first solve the requirements and then proceed with the installation to avoid issues in the future.

For now, we're good with the deployment of Runbook Servers from the Deployment Manager. Now let's see how we can deploy Runbook Designers.

Now, let's assume that we're deploying the new Runbook Designer into a workstation. To deploy a Runbook Designer into a colleague's workstation that will be creating and deploying Runbooks, we'll need only the computer name, permissions for the account executing the task, and to be sure that the prerequisites for the Runbook Designer are met before the deployment.

So, once again, we start at **Deployment Manager**, right-click on the **Runbook Designers** container, and select the option **Deploy new Runbook Designer** just like the screenshot that follows:

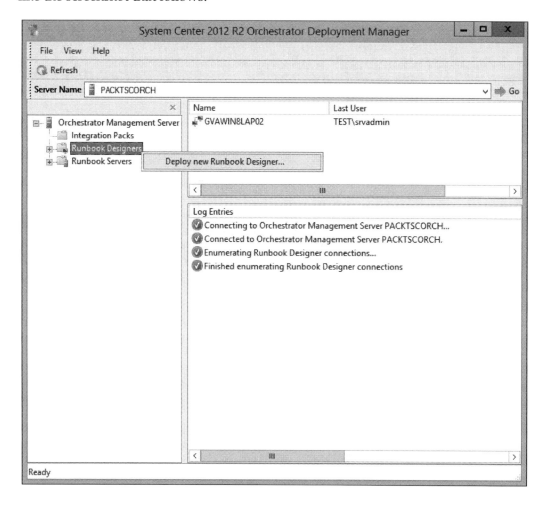

This will trigger the initial wizard screen that you can ignore and proceed to the next one, that is the **Computer Selection** screen, where you can place the name of the workstation (or multiple workstations) into which you're deploying the Runbook Designer. Once filled, press **Next**.

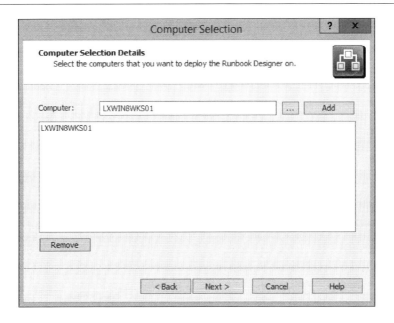

Now, this brings us to the point of **Integration Pack or Hotfix Deployment**, where we'll select the Integration Packs that we'll deploy along with the Runbook Designer into the workstation(s) of our colleagues. In this case, let's say that our colleague's responsibility is for Active Directory, and therefore, he'll need AD and SCOM in order to provide some automations for triggered actions on SCOM (for example) and automate some Active Directory functions as well.

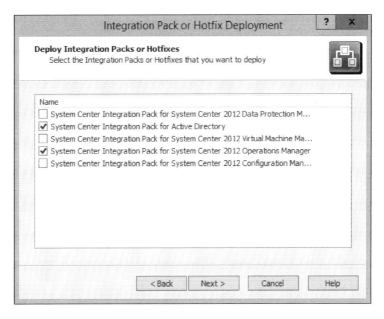

As in the previous examples, this brings us to the confirmation screen of our actions, where we'll press **Finish** to proceed.

In the end of the operation, we can verify the good execution of it by analyzing the **Log Entries** and by checking in the **Runbook Designers** container for the newly installed workstation. The result should be similar to the following screenshot:

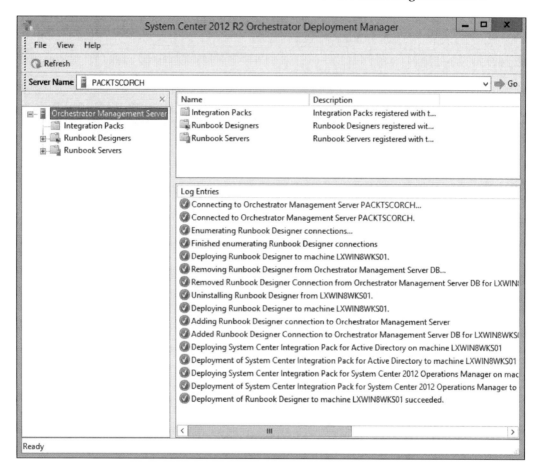

The Deployment Manager can be used to deploy new Runbook Servers or Runbook Designers, and even Integration Packs, but it can also be used to remove them!

In order to remove an Integration Pack from a Runbook Designer (for example, the process is exactly the same on the Runbook Server; we just need to go to a Runbook Server instead of the Designer) we need to proceed as follows.

We start by going into our **Deployment Manager**, browse into the **Runbook Designers** container, and expand it. Then select the Runbook Designer workstation/ server from where you want to remove the Integration Pack, and right-click on the one you want to remove (let's say it was SCOM), and select the option **Uninstall Integration Pack or Hotfix...**.

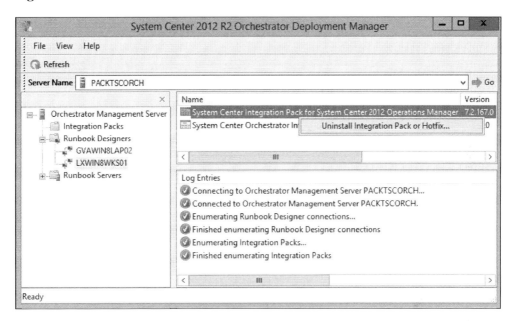

A message will pop up requesting confirmation and indicating the workstation name. Press **OK**, and the operation will proceed.

In the end, you'll see the removal status under **Log Entries** and you'll no longer see the Integration Pack listed in that **Runbook Designer** list, just like in the following screenshot:

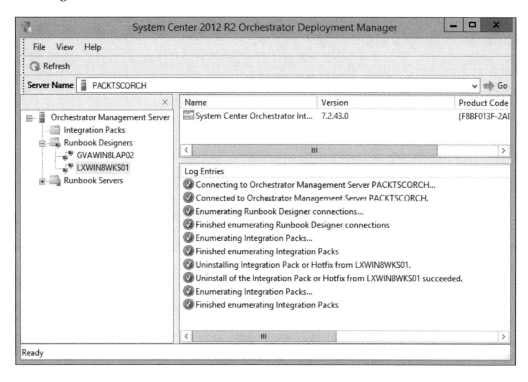

Now, let's imagine that we're decommissioning one Runbook Server and we want to do a clean removal from our Orchestrator architecture. In order to achieve this, we'll have to perform the following tasks in the following order:

1. Uninstall the Integration Packs.
2. Uninstall the Runbook Server component from the server.

To achieve the desired result, uninstall all the Integration Packs from the Runbook Server following the previous procedure, and then right-click on the Runbook Server and select **Uninstall Runbook Server**, as in the following screenshot.

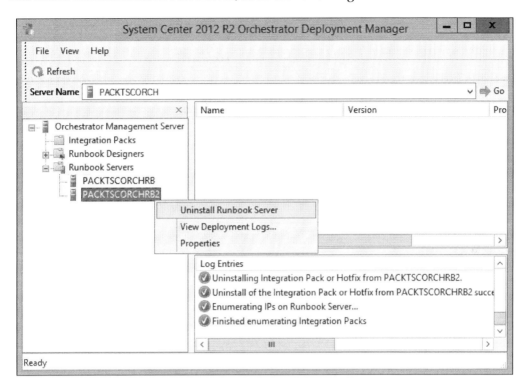

You'll then receive a confirmation message about the uninstallation and its effects, and in that message, you'll also see that the Integration Packs won't be removed for you, but that's ok, you will have removed them before doing this operation, so it won't be an issue.

Now, click on **OK** in the message box to proceed.

You'll then receive another message that contains very useful information, as in the following screenshot:

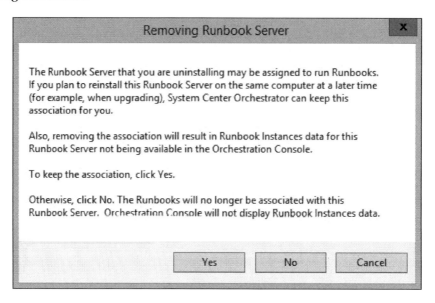

This window gives you the option of keeping existing Runbooks associated with this Runbook Server, and even to keep the records, useful when, for example, you're just upgrading the OS of the server or reinstalling it for some reason.

If you're decommissioning the server completely, you're advised to click on **No** in this window.

For the sake of this exercise, let's say we're decommissioning completely, so we'll click **No** and the removal process will start immediately.

At the end of the removal, as usual, it's possible to check the status of the steps executed in **Log Entries** on the **Deployment Manager** window.

To finish the Deployment Manager part, you can access some useful information from the console. You can access the properties of either Runbook Designers, Runbook Servers, or even the Integration Packs.

The information available in the case of the Integration Packs is accessible by right-clicking on **Integration Pack**, from which we would like to see the information; select **Properties**, and we'll have access to a **General properties** tab that will show us a brief description and the version. Right next to it, there's another tab called **Integration Pack** that will instantly show you where the Integration Pack is installed. Usually, you'll have to click on the **Resolve** button in order to obtain the information.

In the same way, there are properties of the Runbook Designer that will show you the same information on the **General** tab, and it also has a **Runbook Designer** tab that will detail the installed version, the date when it was installed, and the installed **Integration Packs or Hotfixes**.

Now, in the right-click menu of **Runbook Designer**, you'll also find **View Deployment Logs** that will show you the **Available log files** – related entries of all the products installed on that Runbook Designer. This is quite useful if you need further information on how the installation of a certain part occurred.

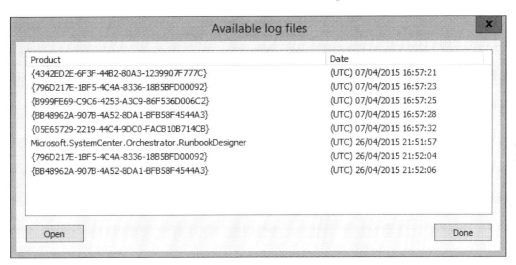

By selecting one of the **Product** ID codes and clicking on **Open**, you'll be able to see the detailed log of that product installation.

This menu is the same for **Runbook Servers** as well.

Now, with this, we've basically covered all the essentials of the Deployment Manager component of Orchestrator, and you'll be able to work with it without a hiccup.

Regarding the troubleshooting of the Deployment Manager or the related deployment of any part contained in it (Integration Pack, Runbook Designer, or Runbook Server), as long as you have the prerequisites installed on the target machines and proper permissions (don't forget the firewall), you won't hit an issue. If you have an issue deploying something from the Deployment Manager, your problem is most probably lack of permissions, firewall, or some missing prerequisite.

The Orchestrator Integration Toolkit

The Orchestrator Integration Toolkit is a set of tools that helps you to create new integrations for Orchestrator. Using wizard-based applications, you can easily create new workflow activities and Integration Packs that extend the capabilities of the product. You can also create custom workflow activities using the Orchestrator SDK and C#, and then package them into an Integration Pack using this toolkit.

This toolkit is composed of four components:

- **Integration Toolkit .NET Integration Pack**: This is needed to run compatible .NET assemblies directly or invoke and/or monitor .NET

- **Command-Line Activity Wizard**: This defines activities that run from CMD and SSH and package to .dll or into a new Integration Pack

- **Integration Pack Wizard**: This allows you to create a package of compatible assemblies and dependent files into an Integration Pack

- **Integration Toolkit SDK Library**: This is used mainly by developers to write custom activities

The platform you're going to integrate with Orchestrator recurring to the Integration Toolkit has to support some types of APIs.

The Integration Toolkit is usually deployed on the developer's machine that will be developing new integrations for Orchestrator to work along with the existing platforms. So, with this in mind, let's look at the following requirements:

- **RAM**: 1 GB

- **Disk**: 60 MB

- **CPU**: Intel Pentium 4 2.4 Ghz / Intel Core 2 Duo 2.0 Ghz or equivalent

- **OS**: Windows 7 or above / Windows Server 2008 R2 or above

- **Software**: .NET Framework 3.5 SP1 and Windows Installer XML Toolset (WiX) version 3.5 specifically

> You can install the Integration Toolkit without the .NET Framework 3.5 SP1, but some operations in the Command-Line Activity wizard will fail if it's not present. Ensure that the .NET Framework 3.5 SP1 is installed before proceeding with the installation.

Here, we'll address how to implement the Integration Toolkit. As for how to develop new activities and even Integration Packs, that goes beyond the scope of this essentials book.

One of the strongest prerequisites of the Integration Toolkit is actually the Windows Installer XML Toolset (WiX) that has to be installed previously. Actually, if you try to install the Integration Toolkit without the WiX installed, you'll receive an error message saying that you need to install the WiX first.

You'll need to deploy a very specific version of the WiX that is the 3.5. No other version is supported, and won't be detected by the Integration Toolkit installer, so be sure to download the proper one from `wix.codeplex.com`.

Once you have the `.msi` file to install, you can start the installation. If you don't have Visual Studio 2005, 2008, or 2010, you'll receive a warning concerning the WiX prerequisites like this one:

This means that only the WiX project and editor package for Visual Studio won't be available, but you'll still have the Command-Line Activity Wizard and the Integration Pack wizard, which we are trying to install.

The rest of the WiX installation is pretty straightforward with the acceptance of the license agreement, proceeding with the installation, and finishing with a completion message.

After this, we can install the Orchestrator Integration Toolkit.

We proceed with **Next**, accept the license agreement, and click on **Next** again.

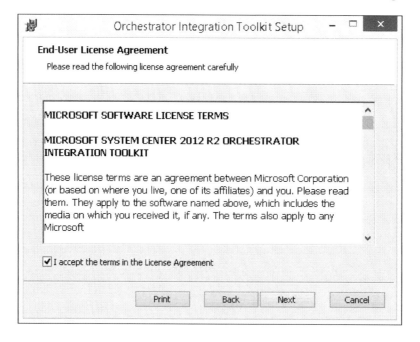

Here, we give our **Full Name** and **Organization**:

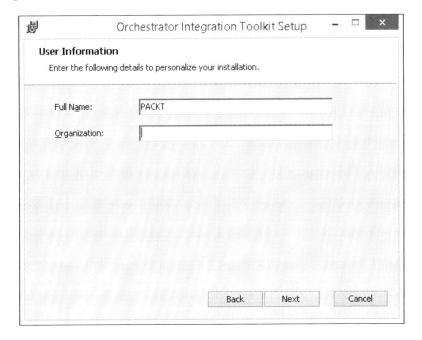

Then, we proceed with the installation:

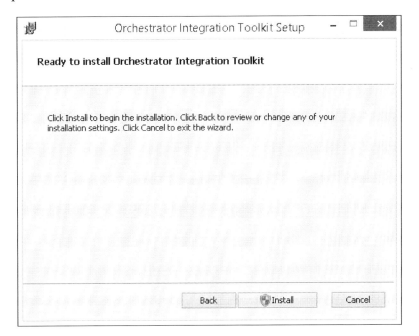

At the end of the installation, we're greeted with a successful installation summary, with the location of the Integration Pack, and now, as we observe in the message, we're going to use the Deployment Manager to get the Integration Pack connected to Orchestrator.

Now, on the first installation of the Orchestrator Integration Toolkit, you'll have to deploy the Integration Pack for testing custom activities. This Integration Pack will have to be delivered to Runbook Designers that have the Integration Toolkit installed.

So, to get the Integration Pack, go to `C:\Program Files (x86)\Microsoft System Center 2012 R2\Orchestrator\Integration Toolkit\Integration Packs` and copy `OrchestratorDotNet.oip` into the Management Server.

After that's done, register the Integration Pack and deploy it into the Runbook Designer that needs it. Once done, you'll find activities related to the Integration Toolkit in the **Activities** pane.

This is as far as we'll go in this book with the Integration Toolkit, as it is a very deep and expanding subject, and goes beyond the essentials for this tool.

The web service

Let's now go around the web service of Orchestrator 2012 R2.

Although this service might be useful for the Infrastructure management team, this is really a service that developers should be aware of and looking at.

This web service is a REST-based service that exposes Orchestrator resources and data through the **Open Data Protocol (OData)**. You can access the web service using languages such as C# and/or scripting languages such as Windows PowerShell.

The service is accessible through an URL (`http://packtscorchw:81/Orchestrator2012/Orchestrator.svc/`) that will show you an XML-formatted website (refer to the following screenshot) with the Orchestrator resources available through the web service.

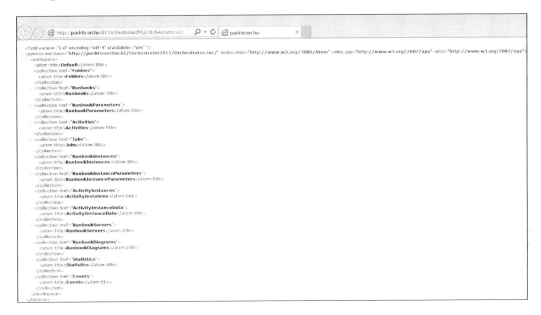

You can also use this website to test whether the service is running.

With this web service, you can execute a few tasks:

- List Runbooks
- Start Runbooks
- View and Stop Jobs
- View Event Logs

You can also call the logging information for those Runbooks from the database through the web service. To achieve this, you will use the GET and POST operations, which will give you a response in the AtomPub XML format.

If you would like to pass more information about this web service to your development team, you can do so by visiting the Microsoft website at `http://msdn.microsoft.com/en-us/library/hh921675.aspx`.

Summary

You're now able to extend your Orchestrator architecture solution to the various platforms and services that you own in your infrastructure. You can also guide and give further pointers to those that seek some way to develop actions and automations to be integrated into Orchestrator, either for in-house applications, or third-party solutions that need automation to become more autonomous.

You will also be able to provide a platform for your developers to contribute to the Orchestrator's success in your organization.

We've lightly addressed the components that are more related to developers' interface (such as the web service), and that is, because after this point it's no longer an essential subject, but yet a completely related programming subject that drifts into something that won't interest the target audience of this book for now.

5
Runbook Examples

This chapter is all about Runbook examples and will get you started on their creation process. Along the course of this chapter, you'll be taught how to address and connect all the pieces together in order to successfully create a Runbook. The creation of a Runbook is driven by the need of it, and it is a process that will require your expertise and knowledge of the technology for which you're creating the automation. You'll find that the knowledge acquired in the previous chapters will all come together now.

It's very important that you weigh the need of the Runbook you're creating versus the time spent on it and the real need of having it (business-wise).

We're going to cover the following topics:

- Runbook for Active Directory User Account Provisioning
- Runbook for Active Directory User Password Reset
- Runbook for Automatic System Log Archiving
- Runbook for Workstations Power Saving
- Runbook for Weekend Maintenance Routine

For the creation of each Runbook, we'll propose a scenario from which we're going to structure our need and come up with a solution. Remember that the creation phase of the Runbook (or the design phase of it) can be very different from person to person, or quite similar. It all depends on how you structure the idea and build the workflow in your mind (or on paper); so keep in mind that good, initial planning is key for a fast development and deployment of your Runbooks.

To move on with the creation of these Runbooks, you'll need to import the Active Directory Integration Pack; so if you haven't installed it yet, please do so before continuing.

Ready!? Let's dig in!

Runbook for Active Directory User Account Provisioning

Now, for this Runbook, we've been challenged by our HR department to come up with a solution for them to be able to create new user accounts for recently joined employees. The request was specifically drawn with the aim for them (HR) to be able to:

- Provide the first and last name
- Provide the department name
- Get that user added to the proper department group and get all the information of the user
- Send the newly created account to the IT department to provide a machine, a phone, and an e-mail address

With these requirements at the back of our minds, let's see which activities we need to get into our Runbook. We'll place these in steps for this example, so it's easy to follow:

- **First step: Data input**

  So, we definitely need an activity to allow the HR to feed the information into the Runbook. For this, we can use the Initialize Data activity (Runbook control category), or we could work along with a monitored file and read the data from a line, or even from a SharePoint list. But to keep it simple for now, let's use the Initialize Data.

- **Second step: Data processing**

  Here, the idea would be to retrieve the Department given by HR and process it to retrieve the group (the **Get Group** activity from the **Active Directory** category) and include our user (the **Add User To Group** activity from the **Active Directory** category) into the group we've retrieved, but in between, we'll need to create the user account (**Create User** activity from the **Active Directory** category), and generate a password (the **Generate Random Text** activity from the **Utilities** category).

- **Third step: Data output**

  At the very end of all this, send an e-mail (the **Send Email** activity from the **Email** category) back to HR with the account information and status of its creation and inform our IT department (for security reasons) too about the account that has been created. We're also going to watch closely for errors with a few activities that will show us whether or not an error occurs.

Let's see the look of this Runbook from a structured point (and actually almost how it's going to look in the end) and we'll detail the activities and options within them step by step from there. Here's the aspect of the Runbook structured with the activities properly linked between them allowing the data bus to flow and transport the published data from the beginning to the end:

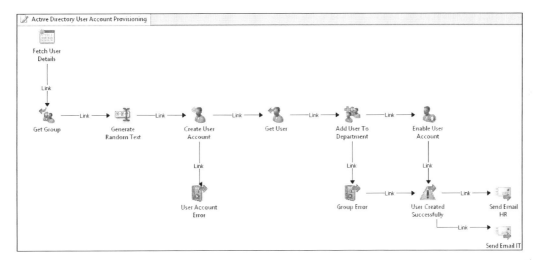

As described in the steps, we start with an **Initialize Data** activity in which we're going to request some inputs from the person executing the Runbook.

To create a user, we'll need his **First Name** and **Last Name** and also the **Department**.

For that, we'll fill in the following information in the **Fetch User Details** activity seen in the previous screenshot:

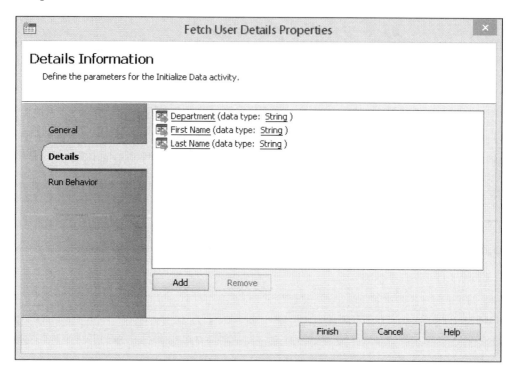

For the sake of avoiding errors, the HR department should have a proper list of departments that we know will translate into a proper group in the upcoming activities.

After filling the information, the processing of the information begins and with it our automation process that will find the group for that department, create our user account, set a password, change the password on the first login, add the user to the group, and enable the account.

For that, we'll start with the **Get Group** activity in which we'll fill in the following:

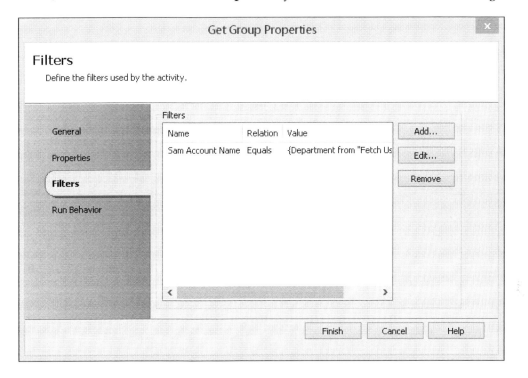

Set up the proper configuration in the **Get Group Properties** window for the Active Directory Domain in which you'll want this to execute, and in the **Filters** options, set to filter **Sam Account Name** of the group as the Department filled by the HR department.

Now we'll set another prerequisite to create the account: the password! For this, we'll get the Generate Random Text activity and set it with the following parameters:

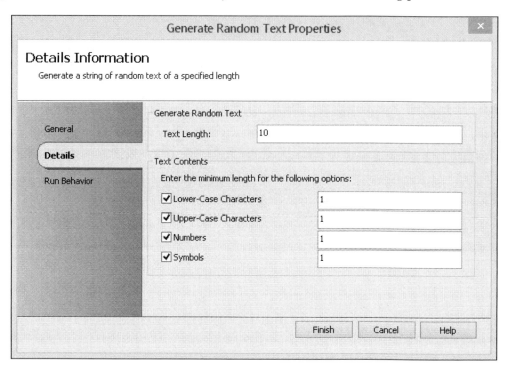

These values should be set accordingly to accommodate your existing security policy and minimum password requirements for your domain.

These previous activities are all we need to have the necessary values to proceed with the account creation by using the Create User activity. These should be the parameters filled in.

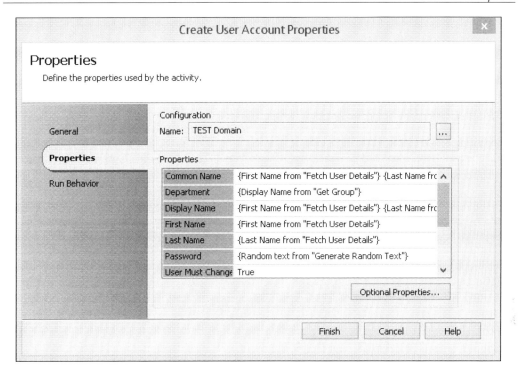

All of these parameters are actually being retrieved from the **Published Data** from the last activities. As the list is long, we'll detail them here for your better understanding. Everything that's between {} is Published Data:

- **Common Name**: {First Name from "Fetch User Details"} {Last Name from "Fetch User Details"}

- **Department**: {Display Name from "Get Group"}

- **Display Name**: {First Name from "Fetch User Details"} {Last Name from "Fetch User Details"}

- **First Name**: {First Name from "Fetch User Details"}

- **Last Name**: {Last Name from "Fetch User Details"}

- **Password**: {Random text from "Generate Random Text"}

- **User Must Change Password**: True

- **SAM Account Name**: {First Name from "Fetch User Details"}.{Last Name from "Fetch User Details"}

- **User Principal Name**: {First Name from "Fetch User Details"}.{Last Name from "Fetch User Details"}@test.local

- **Email**: {First Name from "Fetch User Details"}.{Last Name from "Fetch User Details"}@test.com

- **Manager**: {Managed By from "Get Group"}

As said previously, most of the data comes from the Published Data and we've created subscriptions in all these fields to retrieve it. The only two fields that have data different from Published Data are the **User Must Change Password, User Principal Name (UPN)**, and **Email**. The **User Must Change Password** is a Boolean field that will display only Yes or No, and in the UPN and e-mail we've added the domain information (@test.local and @test.com) to the Published Data.

Depending on the **Create User** activity's output, it will trigger a different activity. For now, let's assume that the activity returns a success on the execution, this will make the Runbook follow the smart link that goes on with the Get User activity.

The **Get User** activity will retrieve all the information concerning the newly created user account that will be useful for the next activities down the line.

In order to retrieve the proper information, we'll need to configure the following in the **Filters** area within the activity:

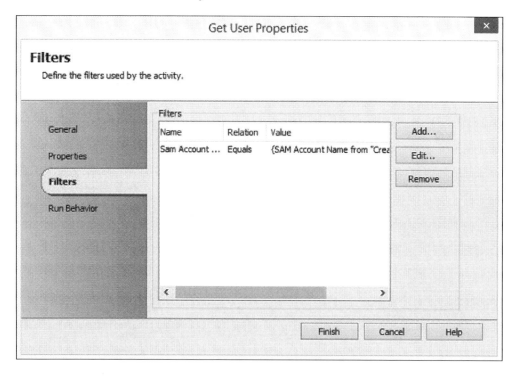

You'll need to add a filter, selecting **Sam Account Name** and **Relation** as **Equals** for **Value** under the subscribed data from **Sam Account Name** that comes out of the Create User activity.

From here, we'll link with the activity Add User to Group (here renamed to **Add User to Department**) and within that activity we're going to specify the group and the user so the activity can add the user into the group. It should look exactly like the screenshot that follows:

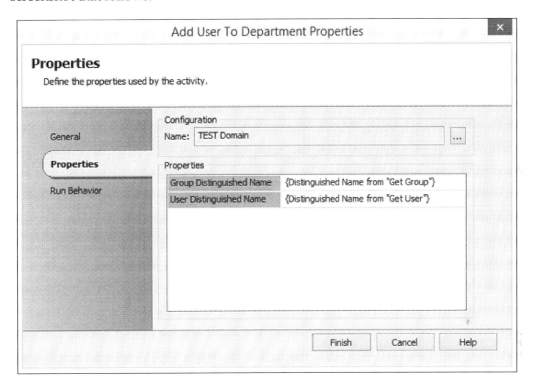

We'll once again assume that everything's running as expected and prepare our next activity, which is to enable user account and for this one, we'll use the **Enable User** activity.

The configuration of the activity can be seen in the next screenshot:

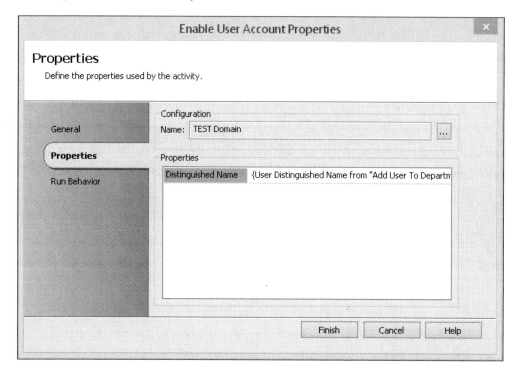

Once again, we'll get the information out of the Published Data and feed it into the activity. After this activity is completed, we're going to log the execution and information output into the platform with the **Send Platform Event** activity so we can see any necessary information available from the execution.

Here is a sample of the configuration for the message output:

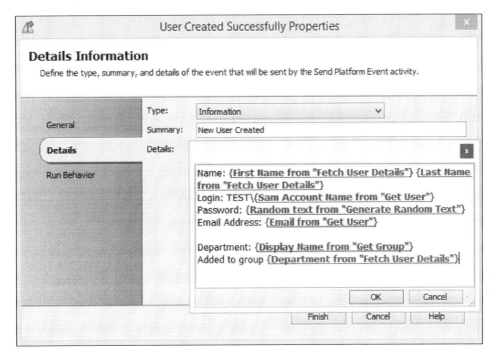

To get the **Details** text box expanded this way, right-click on it and select **Expand…** from the menu, then you can format and include the data that you feel is more important for you to see.

Then we'll send an e-mail to the HR team with the account creation details so that they can communicate with the newly arrived employee and another e-mail to the IT department only with the account name and the department (plus the group name) for security reasons.

Here are the samples of these two activities, starting with the HR e-mail:

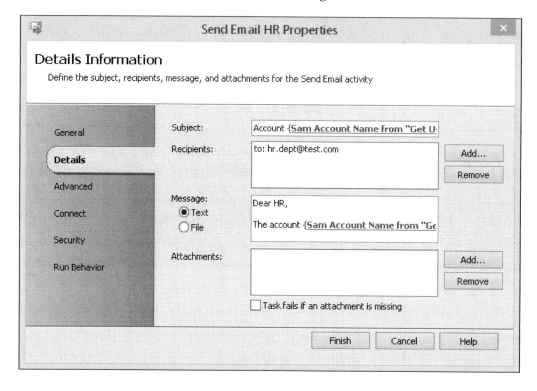

Let's go point by point through this configuration sample.

In the **Details** section, we've set the following:

- **Subject**: Account {Sam Account Name from "Get User"} Created
- **Recipients**: to: hr.dept@test.com
- **Message**: The message description is given in the following screenshot:

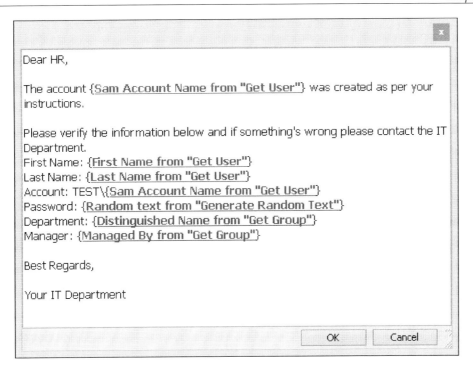

Dear HR,

The account {Sam Account Name from "Get User"} was created as per your instructions.

Please verify the information below and if something's wrong please contact the IT Department.
First Name: {First Name from "Get User"}
Last Name: {Last Name from "Get User"}
Account: TEST\{Sam Account Name from "Get User"}
Password: {Random text from "Generate Random Text"}
Department: {Distinguished Name from "Get Group"}
Manager: {Managed By from "Get Group"}

Best Regards,

Your IT Department

OK   Cancel

Set the **Message** option that consists of choosing the **Priority** of the message (high, normal, or low), and set the necessary SMTP authentication parameters (account, password, and domain) so you can send the message through your e-mail service.

If you have an application e-mail service relay, you can leave the SMTP authentication without any configuration.

In the **Connect** option, you'll find the place to configure the e-mail address that you want the user to see and the SMTP connection (server, port, and SSL) through which you'll send your messages.

Now our **Send Email IT** activity will be more or less the same, with the exception of the destination and the message itself.

It should be something more or less like the following screenshot:

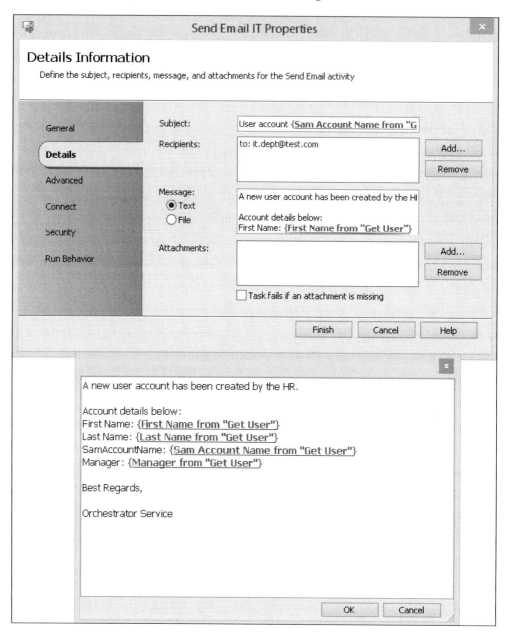

By now you've got the idea and you're pumped to create new Runbooks, but we still have to do some error control on some of these tasks; although they're chained, if one fails, everything fails.

So, for this Runbook, we'll create error control on two tasks that, if we observe well, are more or less the only two that can fail!

One is the **Create User Account** activity, which can fail due to the user account existing or because of some issue with privileges on its creation. The other is **Add User To Department**, which might fail to add the user into the group for some reason.

So for this, we'll create two notification activities called **Send Event** and **Log Message**, which we'll rename to **User Account Error** and **Group Error** respectively.

If we look into the **User Account Error** activity, we'll see something more or less like the following screenshot:

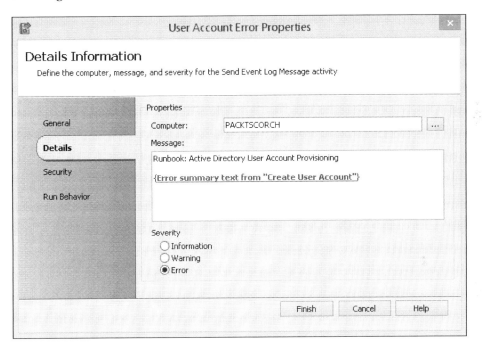

A quick explanation of the settings is as follows:

- **Computer**: This is the computer into whose Windows Event Viewer we're going to write the event into. In this case, we'll concentrate on our Management Server, but you might have a logging server for this.

- **Message**: The message gets logged into the Windows Event Viewer. Here, we can subscribe for the error data coming out of the last activity executed.

- **Severity**: This is usually an **Error**. You can set **Information** or **Warning** if you are deploying these activities to keep a track on each given step.

So, for our **Group Error Properties**, the philosophy will be the same.

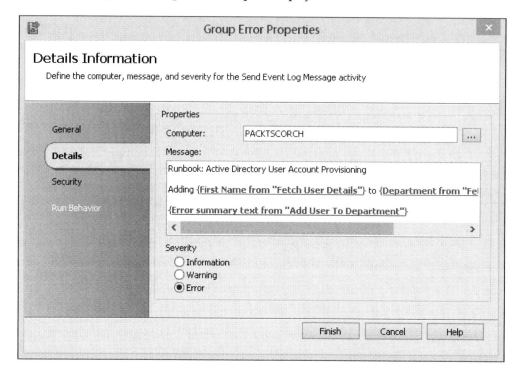

Now that we are all set, we'll need to work our smart links so that they can direct the Runbook execution flow into the following activity depending on the previous activity output (success or error).

In the end, your Runbook should look a little bit more like this:

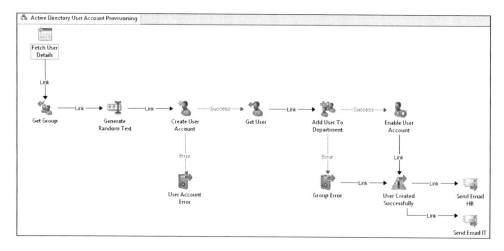

That's it for the Runbook for Active Directory User Account Provisioning. We'll now speed up a little bit more on the other Runbooks as you'll have a much clearer understanding after this first sample.

Runbook for Active Directory User Password Reset

While we're still on the Active Directory activities, we'll target another great sample of automation and process improvement through Orchestrator by speeding up the process of resetting a user's password.

So let's look at the process itself, the design of it and what we need to put in place.

The usual password reset process requires someone from the IT department to be involved at all times, have his Active Directory console open, type the user account to search for it, select the reset password option, define a new password, unlock the account in case the account is locked, and finally communicate the new password to the user.

This process can take up to 2 minutes with an IT helpdesk that has the consoles ready to go and a bit more if he still has to type in his password for his administrative account, open the consoles and so on.

The process with Orchestrator will take under 30 seconds!

Now to the process itself! For the data entry, we'll only need to get the user account and the rest will be automated. At the end, we'll have a Runbook that looks something like this:

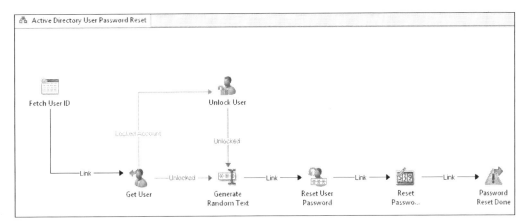

Let's quickly talk about the more common steps and their configuration.

On **Fetch User ID** (Initiate Data activity), we're going to request for the **SAM Account Name** in a string format, and that's the information we're going to use on the **Get User** activity in order to extract all the necessary information, by making a filter for the **Sam Account Name** for the published data coming out of the first activity, and make this Runbook run successfully and serve its purpose.

Now that we've obtained all the information about the account, we're going to create smart links that will have a condition to check whether the account is locked or not, and therefore, execute the **Unlock User** activity if that's the case.

Here's what the smart link will look like when the account is locked:

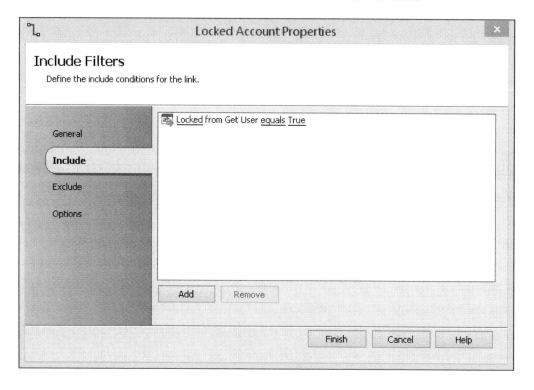

For the locked possibility, we will trigger the **Unlock User** activity; the other possibility (if it's not locked) is that you can either do it by exception from the **Locked** value or basically verify that it's false.

After that, we generate a new password (the **Generate Random Text** activity) and move over to **Reset User Password Properties** in which we'll execute two steps in one; we'll set the password with the value from the previous activity, and we'll set the account for the user to change the password on the next login, just like in the next screenshot:

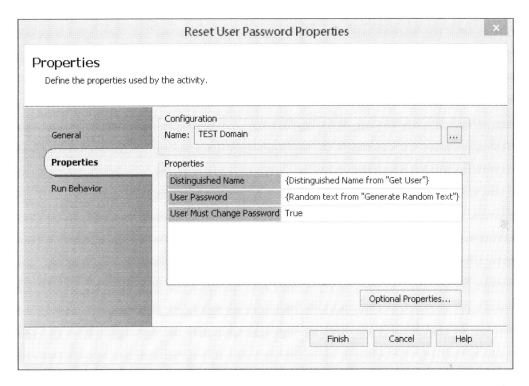

Now, you'll notice that we've set a counter. The counter's objective in this Runbook is actually to give us some statistics on the usage of this Runbook, and therefore, gives us a picture of how much time was saved by using it at the end. This might be useful also if (for example) your helpdesk complains that the password reset activities are a huge demand on them.

The very last activity will then create a notification on the console containing the user's common name and his new password, so you can then transmit it to him in the most appropriate manner.

Runbook for Automatic System Log Archival

In this Runbook, we'll take an example: the need to archive and save space on a server that is identified as having a low disk space or even one that we would like to archive just for historical purposes.

It can also be used just to export the logs from a remote location to the HQ to analyze the logs of a certain server that was reported as having issues or presenting issues; by compressing them, we'll save bandwidth and be able to have a local copy of these logs.

As in the previous example, we'll quickly have an overview of the configurations of the activities in the Runbook, and we'll see how it will look.

This will be your Runbook, once finished:

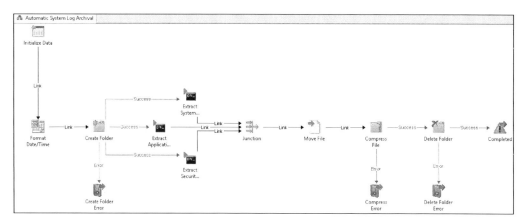

So we start by collecting the computer name from the **Initialize Data** activity and it will be used across our Runbook in multiple activities (such as the **Run Program** activities) so we know where they'll be executed.

Then we'll use the current date to create a temporary working folder into which we'll gather our logs and compact them. In the **Format Date/Time** activity, we'll use a variable called CurrentDnT, defined with the value NOW(), so that it retrieves the current date and time from the system, and on this activity, we'll format it to be used in our **Create Folder** activity to make a difference and avoid overwriting the logs from another system. Also, it will be good if we unpack several archives to do some investigation, and this way we won't overwrite them.

One very important thing to keep in mind is this: **Input Format** changes according to your location. Let's say you're in Europe and most of the countries in Europe use dd/MM/yyyy as the date format; in the US it's MM/dd/yyyy and in other particular cases (such as Switzerland) it is dd.MM.yyyy, so if you detect that your folder doesn't really reflect the **Output Format** you've defined, this might be something to look at.

The configuration of the activity should look like the following screenshot:

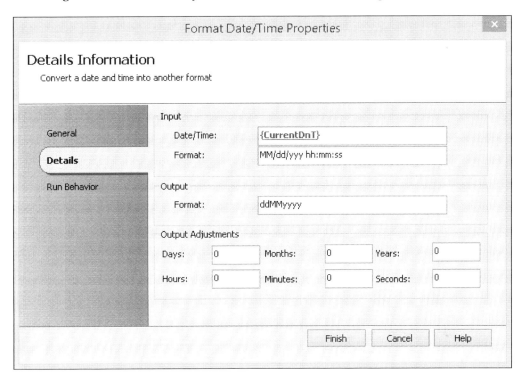

We're then using this formatted information to create our folder by using it at the end of the **Create folder** path, as seen in the screenshot that follows:

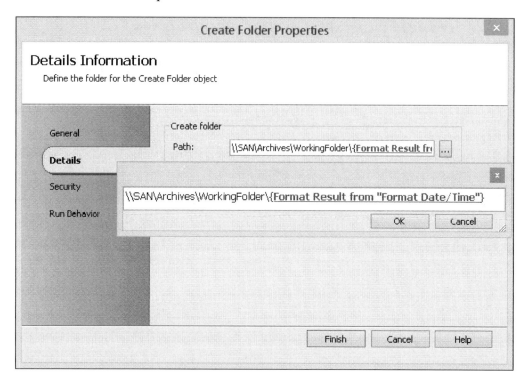

Accordingly, once we've got the folder created, we'll extract the event viewer logs concerning the system, application, and security from the system. This will be stored into the folder with the log file named MachineName-System.evtx (for the system example). To achieve this, we'll use three concurring activities to retrieve each log.

As an example, the **Extract System EventLog** activity will look like the following screenshot:

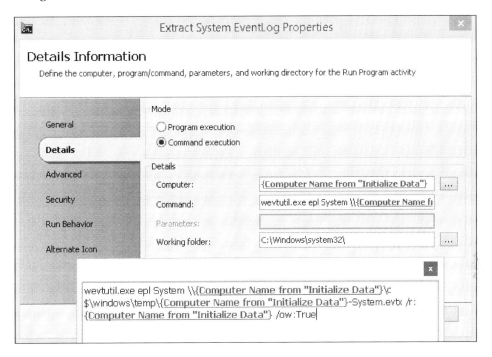

In the previous image, we've expanded the **Command** field so that the entire command will be visible. During the preparation of this Runbook, we've noticed that the extraction of the event viewer logs could be impacted by the local server's UAC and denied due to it. So, as a countermeasure, we locally extract the logs onto the server and then copy them onto the Runbook server to be processed into a ZIP file.

Don't forget that the account used for the Runbook service should have the required permissions to execute the commands/tasks on the server you're targeting.

This could very well be scripted (in .NET or an other language) and we would be using only one activity once, but this is a good opportunity to show you parallel activities and the Junction activity in action.

You will need to change the **System** part of the **Command** field for application and security accordingly in the other two activities.

After these activities, we'll place a **Junction** activity and have it return data from one of the activities so the Data bus continues and we continue to see the published data from the previous activities, and we can use them.

The next step will be to move the files out of our server (from which we're retrieving the logs) onto the machine where we're going to work the logs.

In this example, we've used an archiving share on the storage (as seen in the **Create Folder** activity) in which we gave permissions to the Runbook service account, and you'll see in the next screenshot that we're going to use the output of the **Create Folder** activity to feed the destination folder:

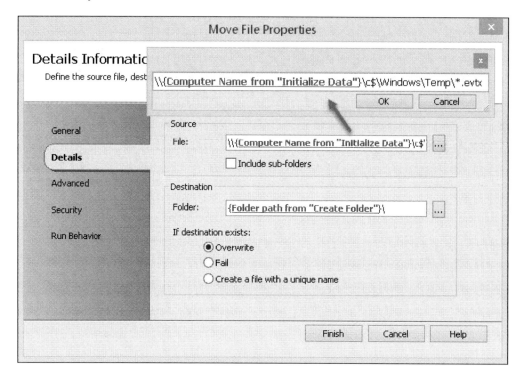

We'll then compact our folder (completely, so we keep a track of the date in the folder name) into a ZIP file directly stored in the storage as seen here:

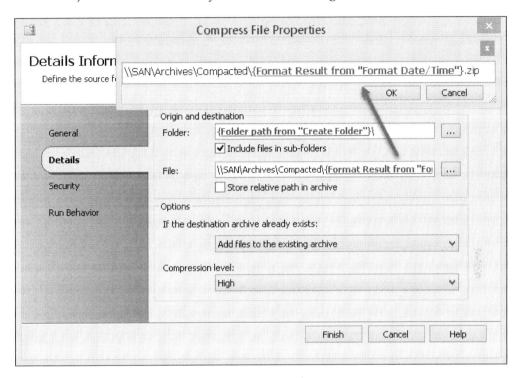

Then, to finish up, we clean up the created folder with everything inside by using the **Delete Folder** activity, and setting the path to {Folder path from "Create Folder"} and the option to delete all files and subfolders.

To conclude, we show an information summary on the console with the details we want.

In this example, we've used the information shown here:

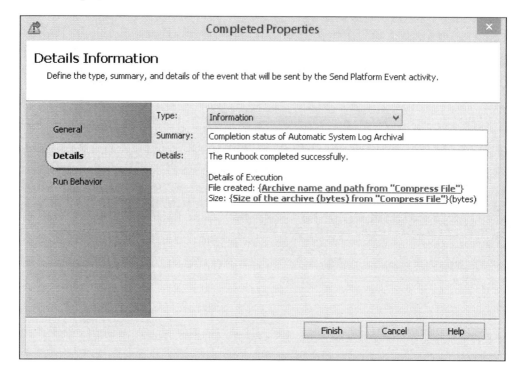

The error activities are only set to show the error summary from the activity that's linked to them and that has a high possibility of having issues.

Runbook for Workstation Power Saving

For this Runbook sample, we will target workstations that are usually left up and running by users during the night, and we'll use it to force those machines to shutdown.

This is a very basic Runbook and works on the assumption that you have a computer group containing a list of machines that are not respecting the outside working hours, or all the workstations in the company.

So, following this example and keeping it in mind, we'll have the following Runbook at the end of this exercise:

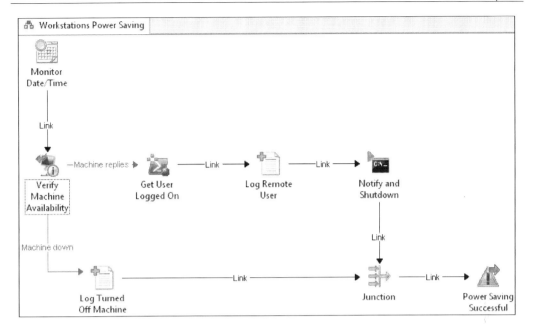

Again, we'll keep it short in terms of explanations as by now, you'll be able to decode what's going on in this Runbook and even design your own just by taking this as a sample for your needs.

We'll start by using a **Monitor Date/Time** activity that we'll configure to be trigged every day at 8:30 P.M., and we'll follow it with **Get Machine Status**, which will verify the machine's availability by ping. This activity will be a subscription of the computer group {Workstations} (in our example) and will run once for each machine.

If the machine doesn't reply, it will be seen as a failure and therefore, will log the turned off machine into a file you specify, and it will then wait for the other branch to complete.

If the machine replies, we'll execute a PowerShell script (actually a single line) to retrieve the user logged at that time in the workstation. This will be achieved by using an **Execute PowerShell Script – Global** activity (which comes in the PowerShell Integration Pack) and using the following line in **PS Script 01**:

```
gwmi win32_computersystem -comp {Computer to ping from "Verify
Machine Availability"} | select Username.
```

It will follow into the **Log Remote User** activity in which we'll configure the log file (txt or log, if you want) and the file encoding (usually ASCII) and the information to be appended in our exercise is in the next screenshot:

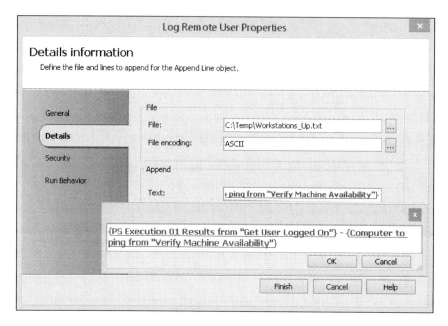

We then create a notification and shutdown action so that if someone's working on that machine, we don't shut it blind and damage the user's work. For this, we'll use a **Run Program** activity and configure it as mentioned in the following sections.

Program execution

To execute the Run Program activity we require the following:

- **Computer**: {Computer to ping from "Verify Machine Availability"}
- **Program Path**: C:\Windows\System32\shutdown.exe
- **Parameters**: -s -f -t 3600 -c (this computer will shutdown in 1 hour. If you're still using it, please cancel this shutdown by typing shutdown -a in a command line)

This will run for each computer that was found active and will then follow onto the **Junction** activity, which will, in turn, flow into the **Power Saving Successful** notification activity.

You can also add an activity to send an e-mail as a *bonus* with the file generated before as an attachment for your local IT staff so that, if a user complains about having lost his/her work, the IT department will know what happened.

Also, another thing that can be done is to execute another parameter to induct the workstation to hibernate (if supported) and that way not damage the user's work.

From here, it completely depends on your imagination.

Runbook for Weekend Maintenance Routine

For our final exercise, let's say you work in a company that typically works from 8:00 A.M. to 5:00 P.M. on the week days and that there's no one working on the weekends. This makes the weekend a very interesting time window for maintenance, and also for cutting costs on power consumption.

We're going to take this opportunity to archive logs and power down workstations on Friday at 11:30 P.M.

The idea of this exercise is for you to take it as a baseline for your own development and experience the nesting of Runbooks.

There's a lot you can then engage into this Runbook, such as updates maintenance, backups of important stuff, and so on. However, all this will really depend on your environment.

For now, let's focus on our Runbook; this is how it will look in the end:

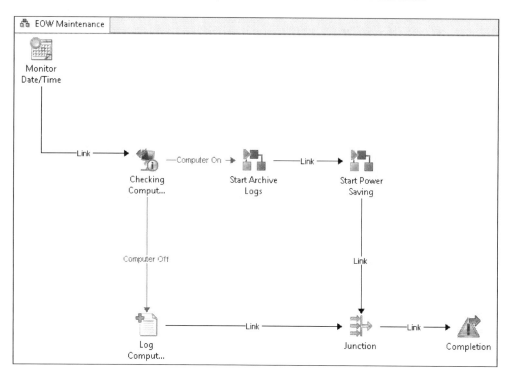

You'll certainly recognize the second path of this Runbook, which is followed if the **Checking Computer Status** activity throws an error, gets logged, and ends in the **Junction** activity. This path was completely extracted from the previous Runbook for **Workstations Power Saving** that we worked on earlier. This is due to the fact that we're going to call that Runbook and therefore, we take the opportunity to check the machines to see if they're up or not before we even call the two Runbooks.

Now, on the **Invoke Runbook** activity, we'll need to pass to the Runbooks the **Computer Name** that we've retrieved from the computer group, which was used in the first activity of the main Runbook. Therefore, we shall configure it accordingly in the activity like in the following screenshot:

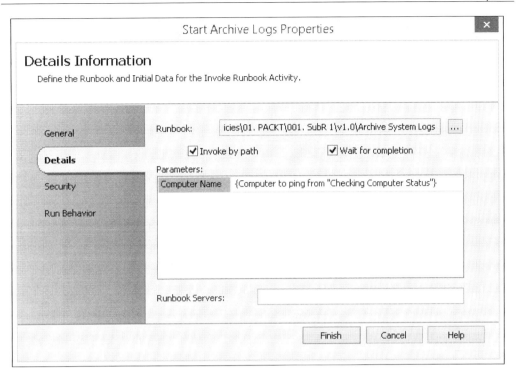

We'll pass down the **Computer Name** parameter and we'll check the **Invoke by path** option and the **Wait for completion** option. It is necessary that each Runbook executes on its own time and not all at the same time to avoid the machine being powered off before retrieving the logs.

The **Invoke by path** option is used to avoid moving this child Runbook into another folder (decommissioning it) and running it anyway.

Now, on the child Runbooks, we've created a copy of the previously created ones into the folder structure (the following screenshot) that we've created. In these, we've proceeded with a few changes to accommodate them and make it possible to integrate them with the parent Runbook:

In the **SubR 1** folder, we'll have the **Archive System Logs** Runbook, in which we've removed the notification activity and replaced it with the **Return Data** activity. Apart from that the Runbook stays the same.

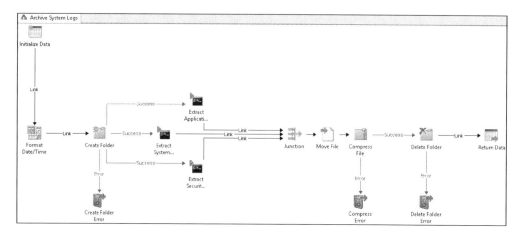

On the **SubR 2** folder, we've placed the **Workstation Power Saving** Runbook, in which we've cut off the error treatment side of it, placed an initialize data activity, and replaced the notification at the end with a **Return Data** activity.

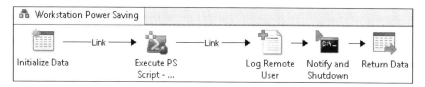

Summary

In this chapter, you've seen some Runbook samples and you should now be able to create a Runbook exploring the possibilities learned in this chapter, such as Junctions, Invoke Runbooks, Counter usage, Parallel activity execution, Error treatment, Notification, and the use of PowerShell and logging.

These Runbooks should serve you as the base for real case scenarios in your environment and help you in the creativity process and also to better understand the configurations necessary for each activity in order to proceed successfully.

Keep in mind that environments are very different from one company to another, and you might find yourself having to explore permissions in depth, such as accounts, and the security configuration on the activities. In an ideal world, you should have your Runbook service account with permissions to execute the tasks wherever it's necessary.

6
Maintaining an Orchestrator Infrastructure

At this stage, you're certainly comfortable with Orchestrator and its components, and you're able to proactively take charge over it and develop new and exciting Runbooks that will provide automation for your environment. However, you might question the High Availability of a service that will become essential in your organization, the security (either delegation or access to information from the various parties involved), the troubleshooting issues or even the backup and recovery.

These are all very important points and valid questions that are raised at this moment when you're fully efficient in developing, deploying, and administrating an Orchestrator solution.

In this chapter, we'll cover the following points:

- High Availability
- Scalability
- Security
- Troubleshooting
- Backup and recovery
- Fine-tuning Orchestrator
- Best Practices Analyzer

The expectation at the end of this chapter is that you can handle an Orchestrator environment without any hassles.

Let's start by addressing the High Availability topic.

High Availability

We need High Availability to ensure that our mission-critical infrastructure components continue to run in case of a failure or unavailability due to maintenance or other operations. The main target of having High Availability is to minimize the impact and downtime of a service; in this case, the Orchestrator service, which you'll be delegating and supporting your operations on, will become more and more critical over time.

For the Orchestrator service to be highly available and able to keep the automation layer of your infrastructure running, you'll need to consider the following factors:

- **Orchestration Database**: You can use either Failover Clustering (SQL Server 2008) or AlwaysOn (SQL Server 2012 and above).

- **Runbook server:** To deploy multiple Runbook servers, you should have more than one deployed in case one of your Runbook servers fail; the Runbooks will be able to run on the next Runbook server, making that way available the execution of tasks.

- **Orchestrator web service and Orchestration console**: Make sure to have multiple load balanced IIS Servers to be able to deliver the console and the web service to continue external access and operations execution. In the case of the load balancing solution, you can either use a hardware solution or the Network Load Balancing solution included in the Windows Server 2012.

- **Management Server**: This component does not need to be highly available because this is only needed when you're deploying Integration Packs, creating or changing new Runbooks, or deploying Runbook Servers.

- **Runbook Designer**: This component, for the same reasons, does not need to be redundant. It will only be useful when creating new Runbooks.

Usually, you won't need a huge setup to keep your Runbooks running peacefully, and you should do fine with a good SQL Cluster (or AlwaysOn) solution, a pair of Runbook servers, and another Orchestrator web service and Orchestration console.

We would advise you to get at least a pair of each of these components that we've just referred to so that you can keep your automations running through maintenance windows (that you might have set for your servers) and through issues that might come up.

Don't forget that if you set a Runbook to run on a specific Runbook server, this Runbook won't run anywhere else. So, if that Runbook server is down for some reason at the time that the Runbook should execute or it's requested by a user, it won't run until the server is back online, as it will be kept on queue by the Management Server.

That said, let's check on the scalability.

Scalability

This question was set here on purpose due to the fact that many people still get confused about scalability and High Availability, even though both topics are quite different from one another. You'll be using High Availability to keep your service available as much as possible during time, thus improving the user experience and also the availability of your service. You'll however, implement scalability to ensure that the service is responding to the service requests (or demand) and therefore, being provided efficiently and in a timely fashion. Don't forget that scalability is used not only to add resources to a service, but also to reduce the service resources, depending on the need and the scope of that same service.

You'll usually start the Orchestrator architecture with a single server deployment to see how it goes and how you can answer the automation requests you'll find. It will be during the technology lifetime that you'll see the demand for this service increasing, making Orchestrator more and more responsible to get automated tasks in place, and you'll see the need for expanding it in order to answer that same demand.

To make sure that you have a clear picture around scalability, and the possibilities that you'll have with Orchestrator, we'll start by drawing a scenario.

Let's say that you've deployed the Orchestrator in a single server topology including the database, to start working with it (or even to follow this book) and in the meantime, it got noticed in your organization and is getting more and more demands for automation and integration with other technologies you have available.

Now, having everything, all of your eggs in one basket, might not be the best idea in this situation, so you might start looking for a solution to distribute the load and (while making your system more available—High Availability) make the system more performant, as the number of Runbooks and requests have changed quite a bit.

In the next diagram, we'll have a look at the orchestrator components in a single server (bubble) and we'll work from there to scale up to a distributed installation.

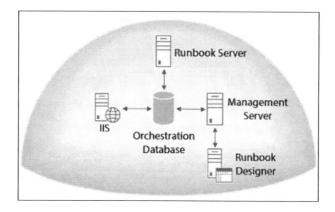

Now, in this scenario, we'll start to address our **Orchestration Database**, and we'll need to either add a node and configure it as a cluster, or move to an existing one that you might already have hosting all your production databases and is therefore, very performant.

In the end, this will mean that our **Orchestration Database** will move elsewhere and we'll lose connectivity between IIS (Orchestration console and web service), **Runbook Server**, and **Management Server**, that we'll need to restore as the next diagram illustrates.

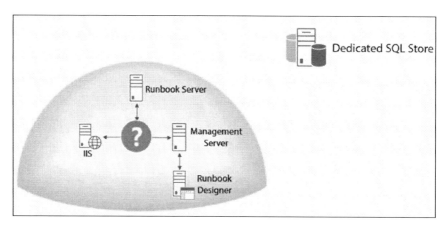

To get this done, we'll need to use the **Data Store Configuration Tool** that comes with Orchestrator. This allows you to configure the **Instance, Server name, Database name**, and **Credentials**. This tool essentially modifies the settings.dat file that is created during the Backup and Recovery tasks that we'll address later in this chapter.

After you've successfully reconfigured the connections, your Runbook server and Management server will reconnect to the database. However, the IIS (specifically, the web service component) will still be *lost*, and in order to have it reconnected to the database, you'll need to reconfigure its `web.config` file of the web service.

With these steps, you'll have a redundant, up-to-scale database that can take the increased load.

But what about the other components? Well, let's address another very important component of Orchestrator that is the Runbook server.

To be sure that the Runbook server will be able to sustain the increased load, you'll have to complete some actions.

You should start by deploying multiple servers, and then deploy the Runbook server component into those servers (with the help of the Deployment Manager from the Management Server).

After that, you can make **Load Distribution and Throttling** by dividing between Runbook servers the more and less demanding Runbooks.

Let's imagine that you have 100 very demanding Runbooks (in terms of load) and 50 less demanding Runbooks; in this case, you could split 50 plus 25 between servers (assuming that you'll have two to start with), reducing the stress on the servers and allowing the load to be shared between them. On top of that, you should configure throttling and prioritization based on the hardware you have available (VM or physical, you should address it as well).

Now, switching into IIS, you can address the scalability for the web service and the Orchestration console, as you would with any other IIS application, which means by using multiple servers with load balancing between them (either hardware or OS based), you can take advantage of some application pool tweaks if you're at ease with IIS at that level.

The **Runbook Designer** is also something that can be scalable by deploying it locally into the workstations of the Runbook designers. This will avoid creating heavy loads over the server and will make this more performant as tests are running locally on the **Runbook Designer** workstations.

The **Management Server**, as we've addressed previously, is a component from Orchestrator that's not extensible, so that's the only component that will always be single in the architecture.

With this, you should be able to scale your Orchestrator architecture in order to answer the requests from your environment.

Security

As in any other tool or technology present in your environment, Orchestrator also has a security layer that can be worked and defined to avoid unauthorized access or prevent the misuse of Runbooks or the service.

Until this point in this book, you've seen which firewall ports to configure for Orchestrator to work and communicate properly, which service accounts to set and for what reason in Active Directory, and even which security groups to create in order to segregate the service access and rights for execution of tasks within Orchestrator, or execution of Runbooks.

Within the Runbooks, you might find yourself having to include or insert passwords for certain activities to execute, and therefore, leaving those passwords in plain text. We discourage you to do so, and instead to use the *encrypted variable* functionality so that you can protect that sensitive information.

Regarding the Orchestrator access, we've defined three types of groups in *Chapter 1, Configuring and Deploying Orchestrator 2012 R2*, to allow a more segregated access to our Orchestrator architecture, and you can use them to fine-tune the permissions by defining who has access to what. As you know, the extension and sensibility of the subject security is quite big and it's not something we can debate in a few lines. Also, isn't the objective of this book to focus on that subject? So, the definition on how and where you're going to apply the groups created previously is completely up to you and your organization.

You can set granular security on **Runbook Folders** and **Runbook Servers**. To do so, it's enough to right-click on the object you want to set the security and set it accordingly, as you can see in the following screenshot:

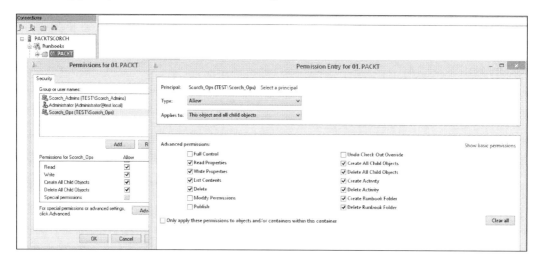

This will allow you, for instance, to give permissions for Runbook authors to change the Runbook content and for normal users to execute that Runbook without the possibility of changing it.

In the same way as we advised you to not disable the firewall in case the communication isn't working between servers or components, we advise you as well to take good care of permissions concerning the Runbooks and who has access to alter them or execute them.

Another thing worth nothing is that as all Orchestrator administrators are part of the **OrchestratorUsersGroup**, all Orchestrator service accounts are members of the **OrchestratorSystemGroup** in an Active Directory.

If you are really working in a secure environment and security is primordial (we are trying to find a reason why it shouldn't be), you can even encrypt the database and communication between servers and the database. For more information about this part, please refer to this link `http://technet.microsoft.com/en-us/library/hh912315.aspx`.

Troubleshooting

This might be the trickiest part of any IT administrator's, system engineer's, or even architect's job (when it really goes south). You might see yourself in a pickle from time to time with a Runbook that's not delivering the expected result or that by some sort of hazard is not running at all.

When troubles come, troubleshooting steps in, and you need to know where to find the good and valuable information that will help you solve the issue on hand.

This information might also be useful to share with the IT administrator's team that you might have in your company so that they can also proactively investigate and solve any issue that might come along.

Troubleshooting in Orchestrator operates in common sense and there's no real magic around it. Usually, if a Runbook fails, it's either because of permissions, account expiry, or a service that changed from one server to another (such as an upgrade, for example).

Let's check the list of steps that you should give while troubleshooting an issue around in Orchestrator.

We can start by checking the Runbook Designer Logging pane that will allow us to check the Orchestrator components' status as well as the Runbook's status and figure out what the issue is in case of an error or warning. This information is stored in the Orchestrator database.

The next logical verification would be to verify that all the Orchestrator services are running properly. Here's a list of them:

- Orchestrator Management Service
- Orchestrator Runbook Server Monitor
- Orchestrator Runbook Service
- Orchestrator Remoting Service

These should be up and running, especially the first three on the list. If these fail to start, make sure the logon credentials of the service are good and not expired. This is the main reason why it's good to have service accounts with complex passwords and to set them such that they do not expire. Make sure that those passwords are not of public awareness and are safely stored.

Now, during the installation of Orchestrator, if something goes wrong, take a good look at the installation logs within the path `C:\Users\<USERNAME>\AppData\Local\SCO\LOGS` and open them using a text editor to verify what's wrong.

There's also another interesting logging possibility called Audit Trails; don't mix this up with the audit history tab on Runbook Designer, it's quite a different subject. Audit Trials provide information about the interaction of a Runbook with external tools and systems as the Microsoft documentation specifies; you can use this to report on configuration, change compliance of processes, and identify changes that are made to non-Microsoft systems for auditing purposes or to remediate a change that causes a service failure.

Since this feature occupies a significant amount of disk space, it's not enabled by default. In order to enable it, on the Management Server, you'll need to do the following:

1. Go to `C:\Program Files (x86)\Microsoft System Center 2012 R2\Orchestrator\Management Server`

2. Run a command prompt from that location as an administrator and run the command `atlc /enable`

3. Grab the logs at `C:\ProgramData\Microsoft System Center 2012\Orchestrator\Audit`

After concluding the troubleshooting, if you'll like to disable the Audit Trails, you can do so by executing the command (at the same location as instructed to enable it) `atlc /disable`.

For further troubleshooting, we have Trace Logs that can give you information and help you identify problems with your environment. By default, they're only written when the Management Service throws an exception, but you can change that by modifying the registry settings. In order to do so, you'll need to go to the registry path (`HKLM\SOFTWARE\Wow6432Node\Microsoft\SystemCenter2012\Orchestrator\TraceLogger`) and you'll need to change the LogLevel key that's usually set to `1` by default. You can increase it to `3` for logging exceptions and warnings / errors or `7` for logging everything (verbose mode).

Keep in mind that logging everything will consume a lot of disk space as everything is logged, so we advise you to keep this to `1` as set by default.

To consult the logs, go to the folder `C:\ProgramData\Microsoft System Center 2012\Orchestrator`.

This concludes the basis of troubleshooting Orchestrator and is more than enough to cover issues that you might come across in your environment.

Backup and recovery

As with any other software in your organization, you'll need to make regular backups of your Orchestrator environment, and once in a while, we suggest you to also verify that the recovery from those backups works as expected. It's always good to have peace of mind regarding this, so we're going to guide you to have a properly functional backup of your Orchestrator environment without doing it completely unaware.

For a complete Orchestrator backup, you'll need to address the following components:

- Orchestration Database
- Management Server
- Runbook Server
- IIS (Orchestration console and web service)

Let's start with the backup of the **Orchestration Database** that, as you might recall, is where everything is stored. There's only one catch when backing up the database, that is, you must backup the **Service Master Key** as well from the SQL Server. This will be required when you're recovering the Orchestration Database on a different, or the same, server after the Service Master Key has been changed.

If you're not sure of what this is or how to backup, you should discuss it with your DBA.

For security reasons, the database and Service Master Key should be stored separately.

Now, moving on to the Management Server, a file backup will suffice as an important part of it to be backed up is the settings.dat file that keeps crucial information from your unique Management Server.

The rule is the same for the Runbook Servers and IIS servers that you have in your environment, meaning that you'll have to get a file backup of each of them and `settings.dat` along with the `web.config` file in the case of the IIS servers.

The `settings.dat` files contain the configuration details required to connect to the Orchestration Database, while the `web.config` file in the IIS servers contain information, as well as knowledge of how the service connects to the database and how the Orchestration console connects to the service. So, the backup of all these parts is crucial for a successful restore of your Orchestrator environment in case of a disaster or critical failure.

Orchestrator supports VSS backups, which means that you won't have to interrupt the service or shutdown the server in order to make a proper backup, as it will use snapshots provided by the VSS service.

To perform backups, you can use a tool such as System Center **Data Protection Manager (DPM)** that comes along with the System Center Suite, and if you actually use it, you can use a tool that comes with Orchestrator that's called `SCOExpressWriter.exe`. This is a command tool that registers an Orchestration Database as a component associated with the Management Server enabling the DPM to backup the database automatically when it backs up the Management Server. Otherwise, you'll have to take a backup separately. This tool can be found on `C:\Program Files (x86)\Microsoft System Center 2012 R2\Orchestrator\ Management Server`.

Fine-tuning Orchestrator

We're now going to address a few common changes on Orchestrator that will help you improve your performance and experience with Orchestrator.

To start, we'll address the Runbook Server Throttling. By default, a Runbook server can run a maximum of 50 Runbooks in parallel, and this number can be changed to better suit your environment requirements or even take full advantage of your servers. You'll see yourself tweaking this to accommodate more or less demanding Runbooks in your system, and due to the impact on the system itself, you might feel the need to increase or decrease the number of parallel Runbooks allowed to be executed.

To do so, you'll need to use the Runbook Server Throttling tool. Navigate to `C:\Program Files (x86)\Microsoft System Center 2012 R2\Orchestrator\ Management Server` and execute a command prompt from there, and in it, the following command (per example: aspt packtscorchrb 70):

```
aspt <RunbookServer> <MaxRunningRunbooks>
```

For the change to take effect, you'll need to restart the Orchestrator Runbook Service in the Runbook server.

You can also tune Runbook server settings in accordance with the execution preference from the Runbook Designer by going to Runbook servers and right-clicking on the Runbook server you would like to tweak, as shown in the following screenshot:

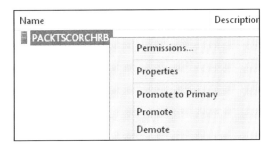

Here, you'll be able to **Promote** or **Demote** a Runbook server in terms of preference for a Runbook execution; except if you've specified where in the Runbook execution it will run, the Runbook itself will start by the higher server in the promotion and go to the next one and so on simultaneously until it finds a slot to execute.

Here, you'll also be able to set **Permissions** on a per user or group basis for Runbook execution, thereby limiting who can execute a Runbook and from where. This is useful when you have a geographically distributed Runbook servers architecture to prevent users from Europe from executing Runbooks in America (for instance).

The Best Practices Analyzer

Now, last but not least, (we've kept this one for the very end because it will make much more sense now) is how to make a good check on your Orchestrator environment and verify that it's compliant with Microsoft recommendations.

The Best Practices Analyzer does not come installed by default with Orchestrator, but it's very useful to have it installed, and we recommend you to do so as a sanity check for your Orchestrator environment.

1. To start with, you'll need to download and install the **Microsoft Baseline Configuration Analyzer (MBCA)** on the Orchestrator Management Server that you can find easily with a quick search on the Internet.

2. Then, you'll have to download and install the `Microsoft. SystemCenter2012.Orchestrator.BestPracticesAnalyzer.msi`.

Once you have this installed and ready, you'll be able to do the following:

- Scan Orchestrator deployment
- Validate against Microsoft recommendations
- Get an extraction of misconfigurations or missed best practices

Once you finish the scan, you'll be able to extract a compliance report that can actually be exported in an XML format that you can process and import wherever you like.

Summary

This concludes our sixth and final chapter on Orchestrator, and now you should be able to troubleshoot, verify, and secure your environment against the best practices and Microsoft recommendations. As this is an essentials book, we've covered the very essentials of each part of Orchestrator, and you are now able to continue to explore and go deeper into the automation world on your own.

Azure services were not covered in this, as well as some other very known and used third-party software, because that would drive off many readers and it would lose the essentials target defined for this book.

We encourage you to use your imagination and explore and make a profit from Orchestrator on a level that you would never imagine, which will help you gain time and reduce repetitive tasks that get boring after a certain time.

Index

security 152, 153
Service Master Key 156
single-server solution
  deploying 7-15
System Center Configuration
      Manager 79, 80
System Center Data Protection Manager 86
System Center Operations Manager 80
System Center Virtual Machine
      Manager 82-85

V

Virtual Machine Manager Integration
      Pack 82

W

web service, Orchestrator 2012 R2 113, 114
Windows Remote Management
      (WinRM) 82

Thank you for buying
Microsoft System Center
Orchestrator 2012 R2 Essentials

About Packt Publishing

Packt, pronounced 'packed', published its first book, *Mastering phpMyAdmin for Effective MySQL Management*, in April 2004, and subsequently continued to specialize in publishing highly focused books on specific technologies and solutions.

Our books and publications share the experiences of your fellow IT professionals in adapting and customizing today's systems, applications, and frameworks. Our solution-based books give you the knowledge and power to customize the software and technologies you're using to get the job done. Packt books are more specific and less general than the IT books you have seen in the past. Our unique business model allows us to bring you more focused information, giving you more of what you need to know, and less of what you don't.

Packt is a modern yet unique publishing company that focuses on producing quality, cutting-edge books for communities of developers, administrators, and newbies alike. For more information, please visit our website at www.packtpub.com.

About Packt Open Source

In 2010, Packt launched two new brands, Packt Open Source and Packt Enterprise, in order to continue its focus on specialization. This book is part of the Packt Open Source brand, home to books published on software built around open source licenses, and offering information to anybody from advanced developers to budding web designers. The Open Source brand also runs Packt's Open Source Royalty Scheme, by which Packt gives a royalty to each open source project about whose software a book is sold.

Writing for Packt

We welcome all inquiries from people who are interested in authoring. Book proposals should be sent to author@packtpub.com. If your book idea is still at an early stage and you would like to discuss it first before writing a formal book proposal, then please contact us; one of our commissioning editors will get in touch with you.

We're not just looking for published authors; if you have strong technical skills but no writing experience, our experienced editors can help you develop a writing career, or simply get some additional reward for your expertise.

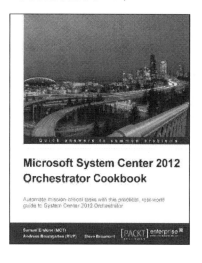

Microsoft System Center 2012 Orchestrator Cookbook

ISBN: 978-1-84968-850-5   Paperback: 318 pages

Automate mission-critical tasks with this practical, real-world guide to System Center 2012 Orchestrator

1. Create powerful runbooks for the System Center 2012 product line.

2. Master System Center 2012 Orchestrator by creating looping, child and branching runbooks.

3. Learn how to install System Center Orchestrator and make it secure and fault tolerant.

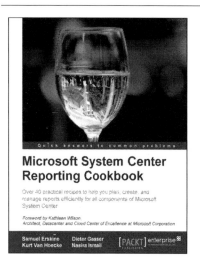

Microsoft System Center Reporting Cookbook

ISBN: 978-1-78217-180-5   Paperback: 358 pages

Over 40 practical recipes to help you plan, create, and manage reports efficiently for all components of Microsoft System Center

1. Create and deliver high value reports to show the value of your System Center investment.

2. Gain access to real world solutions in the art and science of report planning and creation using System Center data.

3. Practical cookbook with recipes that will help you get the most out of Microsoft System Center through the creation of business valued reports.

Please check **www.PacktPub.com** for information on our titles

Managing Microsoft Hybrid Clouds

ISBN: 978-1-78217-716-6   Paperback: 308 pages

Benefit from hybrid cloud scenarios through this detailed guide to Microsoft Azure Infrastructure Services (IaaS)

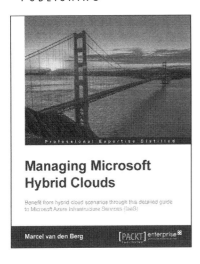

Managing Microsoft Hybrid Clouds

Benefit from hybrid cloud scenarios through this detailed guide to Microsoft Azure Infrastructure Services (IaaS)

Marcel van den Berg

1. A unique and deep insight into the Microsoft Azure Infrastructure Services.

2. Learn how to securely connect your datacenter to Microsoft Azure.

3. A step-by-step guide that explores numerous cloud hybrid scenarios.

Microsoft System Center Data Protection Manager 2012 SP1

ISBN: 978-1-84968-630-3   Paperback: 328 pages

Learn how to deploy, monitor, and administer System Center Data Protection Manager 2012 SP1

Microsoft System Center Data Protection Manager 2012 SP1

Learn how to deploy, monitor, and administer System Center Data Protection Manager 2012 SP1

Steve Buchanan   Islam Gomaa
Robert Hedblom   Flemming Riis

1. Practical guidance that will help you get the most out of Microsoft System Center Data Protection Manager 2012.

2. Gain insight into deploying, monitoring, and administering System Center Data Protection Manager 2012 from a team of Microsoft MVPs.

3. Learn the various methods and best practices for administrating and using Microsoft System Center Data Protection Manager 2012.

Please check **www.PacktPub.com** for information on our titles

68186181R00102

Made in the USA
Lexington, KY
03 October 2017